Working Writer Happy Writer: How to Build a Thriving Writing Business from NOTHING

by Sue LaPointe

Published by:
Triumph Publishing
Triumph Communications, LLC
Port St. Lucie, FL 34984
www.becomeafreelancewriter.com

Second Edition, 2009

ISBN 1441404546

For my husband and best friend –
Thank you for never questioning whether I could do this,
for keeping the wheels on,
for dreaming big with me.

For my children –
Thank you for being the 'best' of the best part of the day.

To God be the glory – great things He has done.

"A world that works for everyone – with no one left out."

Brian Klemmer

Working Writer
Happy Writer

How to Build
a Thriving Writing Business
from NOTHING

by Sue LaPointe

TABLE OF CONTENTS

Foreword

Sue LaPointe came to me unsure of just what she wanted to do... a Network Marketing business or become a writer? Which shall it be? And in her mind, they rated equally. However, it didn't take me long to realize where her true worth would be. After all, my job is to hold the vision of success when the client can't do it for themselves.

When Sue and I finished her coaching program she was well on her way to her monthly revenue goals. In fact, in 6 months she went from zero to $5,000/mo. She is well beyond that now and continuing to grow. Her ability to contribute to her family financially while being home when the kids need "Mom" has been amazing. She controls her time while continuing to expand her business.

As a coach, the powerful question I like to ask is "What happened?"

Several things. Sue was coachable. She was willing to do her "homework" with no excuses. And she was willing to be uncomfortable. Because reaching for your dreams WILL make you uncomfortable. Sue never waivered when I would set her a new challenge of doubling something: Double your income, double your bidding, double the number of clients.

In coaching, I was able to gauge just when she needed the next expanding task. Sue was stretched without being snapped. Each session led to higher quality questions and actions. By the end, she was the master of a working business model that she could grow on her own.

What you are about to read is a roadmap for doing exactly what Sue did. Through her coaching she went from vague to focused. And at each turn, when challenged, she stepped up and developed the necessary systems to expand her capacity as a writer and business owner. Now she is sharing her hard-earned knowledge with you.

This business isn't rocket science. It's a simple business and it's simple to systemize it. Sue's clear writing style makes it very easy to do what she has done. She leaves nothing out. You just have to take action and do your "homework" with no excuses. And if you get stuck, get a coach.

To Your Writing Success,

Robin M Powers – www.RobinMPowers.com

Introduction

A writer?

Hmm.

You want to be a writer? Why not an astronaut? A veterinarian? A ballerina? A movie star?

Those other childhood dreams seem about as likely to happen. So what on earth would make you think you could become a writer – and actually make money doing it?

I mean, look at the odds! How many people do you know who've actually written a book that got published and made money? The chances of writing a book that becomes a bestseller are dismal.

Can't you just imagine some poor writer slaving away for years on this pathetic novel, hoping against hope that some agent or publisher will take a chance? Is that how you want to spend your life?

Ever had that conversation in your head?

I know I did – many times. Right before I read a few books that changed my life.

Just like many of you, I had a certain idea about what it would mean to be a writer. You'd have to write a novel, get it published, and maybe even get the book into Oprah Winfrey's hands to have any chance of success.

Or, you could write a non-fiction book about something kind of obscure – something you know better than anyone else in the world.

Doesn't seem very likely, does it?

So, like many of you, I moved on to the next area of writing. I started reading how-to's about writing articles for magazines and trade journals. I pored over Writer's Market. I found every website out there that gave information about which publications would welcome new writers, how much they'd pay per word, where to find the submission guidelines.

It looked like a really long road ahead.

Lots of query letters to send. Lots of wracking my brain to come up with a unique article that would catch the editors at the right time and place in their editorial calendar. Lots of dead ends. It didn't sound very appealing to me.

So I kept looking.

I don't even remember how I stumbled onto Peter Bowerman's book *The Well-Fed Writer* – must have been in a forum of some kind.

But I ordered it and had one of the biggest a-ha moments of my life. Freelance commercial writing.

Never heard of it. What is that? Writing commercials? Technical writing?

I started reading.

Oh. My. Goodness.

Wait a minute. Is this guy trying to tell me that there are businesses out there – a LOT of businesses - that will pay me to write for them?

YES!

The next book was Robert Kiyosaki's *Rich Dad Poor Dad*. I'm actually kind of embarrassed to say how I came across that one. A friend recommended it, and I thought it was about how to give your kids an allowance wisely – teaching them the right lessons about money.

Eye opening.

The whole idea is basically that wealth is a good thing, and that the biggest way to get wealth is to own a business. Got me thinking.

Next, I read Loral Langemeier's *The Millionaire Maker.*

She really made it look pretty simple. Build a "cash machine" – a business that cranks out money that you can use to make high-return investments. The cash machine is built on your existing skill set – not necessarily your dream business.

Hmmm.

At the back of the book, there was an offer for a free consultation. You could call and get a good picture of where you are, where you want to go, and how you could get there. You could sign up for the one-on-one coaching program, and learn how to build a cash machine of your own.

I called.

I knew this could work. I coughed up the coaching fee, and wondered what would happen next.

My coach was Robin Powers – a perfect match. We discussed a few options, and finally settled on building a writing business.

Then I had the same big question you've probably had already.

"Am I a good enough writer to do this?"

I knew I could string words together. Co-workers had often asked me to proofread or rewrite their letters. I'd even had the honor of having some papers in college and grad school used as samples because the professors liked them.

But was that enough? I'd have to try it and find out.

Then came the next question – and you can probably guess it.

"What if I fail?"

OK, so this would take some courage. It didn't seem like it would cost much – I already had a computer, internet access, and a dictionary. The only thing at risk was really my pride – and my sense of hope.

That was a big one, though. I've had more jobs than I'd like to admit.

- Staff accountant (never felt really good at that)

- Administrative assistant (really fast typist, but usually kind of bored)

- Network marketer for skin care and cosmetics company (never got the hang of that)

- Other failed attempts at selling

  o Hand-knit sweaters for kids and dogs

  o Cigar box purses

  o Sock monkeys (nope, I'm not kidding – I even did some dressed as a bride and groom pair, complete with veil and black hat)

- Counseling intern in a state mental hospital (very scary)

- Medical billing in a family practice office (um, one word – collections)

- Temp agency secretary (new office every week – how do I answer THIS phone?)

- Veterinarian assistant (sometimes fun, often stinky)

- Counter help at a European pastry shop (yeah, croissants smell good at first, but you can't get the smell out of your hair)

You can see where that was all headed.

"What are you going to be when you grow up?" was a question that had dogged me for about thirty years.

If people didn't take me seriously in a new venture, I couldn't blame them. But if I tried a business that really tapped into what I thought were my true talents – and failed – I wouldn't know what else to try.

Like many of you, I settled into a holding pattern while I searched for some courage.

I found it one day after taking a temp job at a non-profit organization. When I arrived, my supervisor told me when my bathroom break would be.

That was it.

As an adult – one with a college degree, nonetheless – I just couldn't justify working at a job where I could only "go" when I had permission. There was the courage I needed!

Maybe you're in the same place.

You might be working at a job that's okay, but really not what you've ever dreamed about. Or, maybe it's not even okay, and you'd leave in a heartbeat if you could find another way to make money. Maybe you have children at home, and want to find something you can do that doesn't disrupt your family life – you want to work when they're at school or napping. Maybe you're retired and want to try your hand at something new or make some extra money – but the idea of being a greeter at WalMart isn't so appealing.

Then this book is for you!

There's a whole world of writing out there that you may never have considered. It's easy to get jobs that pay well. It's never boring. You get to be picky about what you'll write about, and who you'll write for. And you can do it anywhere you've got a computer.

(Now, I really don't recommend the beach – it sounds great on paper, but getting sand out of your laptop, and salt spray off your screen is not good.)

And best of all, you can determine how much you'll make and how much you'll work.

You can definitely go the route of hiring a coach.

I totally recommend it – Robin's input and guidance made a huge difference in my life, and greatly flattened the learning curve. But if you're not in a position to do that, this book may be a pretty good substitute to get you started.

Chapter 1 – Getting Started

Taking the First Step

For lots of businesses, the first step is getting a business plan done.

You've got to go into extreme detail about marketing tactics, performance strategies, personnel, financing, market research results, all that kind of stuff. It's a lot like a cross between doing your taxes and writing a report.

You don't have to do any of that to get going with a writing business.

What you have to do, is to get a gig.

You want to get this thing in motion, and then shape it after it's viable. There's really nothing you've got to spend up-front for equipment, as long as you've got a computer and internet access.

So there's no financing.

When you're starting off, you don't need any employees. You don't have to do any market research, either, because you're about to learn where you can find them – congregating, just waiting for you.

There are just a few things you need to do before you can get your first gig:

1. Get a Paypal account.

2. Assemble a very small portfolio.

3. Get a job board membership.

Paypal

This is a free service where you can get paid online. It's simple to use, but it does take a few days to get activated. Start on it first so you can get paid quickly when the time comes.

Creating the Perfect Portfolio

It's a chicken and an egg situation when you're just starting out. Clients want to see your portfolio before they'll hire you – but you need them to hire you before you can build a portfolio. Right?

Wrong!

And believe it or not, this is one of the biggest, silliest stumbling blocks many wannabe writers trip over. Quitting over this is a classic case of thinking within the box.

What exactly do these potential clients want?

Some of them actually do want to see that you've been published, that you've got journalistic credits and bylines out the wazoo. But that's a sure tip-off that they don't need a freelance business writer – they want a journalist.

And we've already talked about how that's not what we do.

We're not chasing a Pulitzer here – we're helping businesses make money. It's not literary. It's not all that sexy. But it's a sure way to make money – and it's a lot easier to get started.

So cross the journalist-seekers off your list of prospects. What else do these people want to see?

Generally, they want to see that you've done something sort of similar to what they need done. So, if an orthodontist needs a tri-fold brochure, she's cool with you showing her the brochure you did for an appliance repair shop.

The internet marketer who needs SEO articles about digital cameras is usually satisfied when you provide a few articles you did on replica pirate guns.

Mostly they're just looking to see whether you can string some words together into a coherent sentence, whether you will actually follow through and provide these samples, and whether you'll follow directions as you submit a proposal.

Now where do you get these little goodies if you've never gotten a gig before?

From your own brain!

Think about it – how do graphic design students create a portfolio? It's usually based on class assignments for imaginary clients.

The first brochure I ever created was for my chiropractor. I changed all the particulars - since he hadn't actually ever exactly asked for a brochure – but it was essentially based on his practice. I'd gotten great relief for my back by seeing him, and wanted to help his business if I could. I knew I could do better than the brochure he was using.

So I used his facts and invented a fictional doctor to feature in the brochure.

I even showed it to him (putting his own info in) later, but I think he thought I wanted to be paid for unsolicited work.

Oops!

Once we cleared up that misunderstanding, I think he was duly impressed. Of course, he'd written his original feature-driven brochure, and continues to use it (oh well!). In hindsight, the lesson is that it's not necessary (or wise!) to show how you've improved someone's marketing materials – just use the basic facts to give credibility to the sample you're creating.

You can do this for any type of small project – brochures, flyers, print ads, articles, press releases, and sales letters. All you need is a couple of samples to start. Then use your paid projects as you get them.

It's best to provide your samples in PDF format. For example, I use Publisher to create most marketing materials. (It's old. It's antiquated and cumbersome – I know! But it's still easier for me than learning InDesign or some other design software.) One problem with Publisher is that nobody else seems to use it, so they can't open the files to see my gorgeous samples.

That's why a PDF works well.

Pretty much everyone can access a PDF file – and you can mess with the document settings so that nobody can edit or copy your work. It's a lot more secure and professional looking. So as you create your portfolio, save each piece as a PDF. (Don't bother getting an expensive PDF writer – I'll tell you about a free one a little later.)

Keep updating your portfolio when you've got new pieces.

Swap out the old and put in the new docs that show your advanced skills. You could get really nerdy and test your portfolio, and you'd get this thing down to a science. I did this with some sample articles, and know that the ones I send prospective article clients will most likely get me the job.

How and when you send your samples is important, too.

Don't send them until the client requests them. And when you do send them, be sure to follow the client's directions, if they get specific.

They may ask for attachments or for the samples to be pasted into the body of an email. They may ask for links to your portfolio. That's an easy one, because you can just send them to the appropriate page on your website.

Only in one case did a prospect ask for me to physically mail her some samples.

What a pain! I hustled to the post office, paid for postage, and then never heard back – and she's the one who called me!

After a while, you develop a sense for which clients may become more trouble than you want. At this point, if a client were to ask me to mail samples, I'd know right then not to go any further. There are so many projects and clients out there that after a while, you'll be able to be kind of picky about what you do.

Get a Membership on a Job Board

There are several to choose from: Elance, O-Desk, Rent-a-coder, Quality Gal, Editfast, and my favorite, Guru – plus probably a dozen others.

The great thing about these job boards is that they serve as a place where your potential clients line up to find writers who can help them with their needs. You're not out there taking out newspaper ads, making cold calls, pestering your relatives, or showing up on the doorsteps of unsuspecting business people begging for work. They're already right there, telling you exactly what they need.

Some of these sites are free, and some have a small fee for a membership. Of course, even a small fee seems big when you're starting from scratch – but aim to get a paid membership as quickly as you can, by any means! You're very likely to make it back in the very first writing assignment you do.

Be prepared for this, though: You will likely need to place a lot of bids before you get a project. What's a lot? Well, I recommend bidding on at least 5 projects, 5 days a week – more if you can, especially when you're just starting out.

I've read that the universe rewards massive action. It's basically a numbers game, and you'll find yourself writing for money a lot faster if you jump into action rather than just waiting for it to come to you.

Chapter 2 – How to Find Work

Getting Gigs on Job Boards

If you want to start your freelance writing business with training wheels, like I did, you can't beat registering with a job board. There are lots out there, but the biggies are Guru.com, Elance.com, and Rentacoder.com. With some variations, they work the same way: they let people who need something written post their project for writers to bid on.

It's a great way to start, if you do it the right way.

You can do it the hard way, and get frustrated, quit writing altogether, and live under a bridge for the next few years (isn't that a writer's biggest fear? Or, at least your family's biggest fear for you?).

Or, you can do it the easy (easier!) way, and actually get some cash coming in.

I'm not sure how all of the other freelance sites work the payments, but with Guru, you can get direct deposit. Make sure you set that up before you even place your first bid.

It's amazing how motivating it is to click that little button that says "withdraw funds" after you've done a project and gotten paid by a happy client.

Then poof! The money's in your bank account.

Top 10 Tips on Getting Work from Job Boards

Here are ten tips for getting the biggest bang for your buck.

1. **Pay a buck! (or several)**

If you go with the free level of membership, you're in competition with tons of writers – and writers who are (how can I say this nicely?) cheap.

What does this mean for you?

If you're competing against writers who are desperate, they'll underbid you. They're the ones who'll write someone's biography for $50. Frankly, you don't want to compete with them on price. And the type of client you'll get is not what you really want, either.

If you join at the lowest level of paid membership, the herd thins considerably. You're not making a huge investment, but you'll set yourself apart.

For about $30 a month, you'll be on a whole different level. It's almost a guarantee that you'll make the fee back in the very first project you do.

In my case, my first project was a $400 speech – not bad!

Most of the people listing projects open them only to paying members – it's kind of a litmus test for them. So you'll find better projects and less competition for them.

2. **Work on your resume or member page**.

When you don't have any feedback yet, this is all your potential clients have to go on about you.

Make it look good.

Take a look at how other writers do their pages, and follow their example. If possible, link to writing samples or at least offer them. As you get projects, remember to update your information.

3. **Choose a pay range that makes sense.**

Most of these sites offer you several choices. Think long and hard about your hourly rate. Remember how important perception is, too. Would you expect better results from a haircut you paid $7 for or a $70 cut? Never mind that the stylist at the $70 salon may have worked at Super Cuts last week!

I've learned a lot about setting an hourly rate.

When I started with Guru, I set my rate at $28 per hour. Not quite sure why – it just seemed reasonable.

But my hourly rate goal was actually $75 – quite a difference. In order to meet my income goals, $75 per hour was where I needed to aim.

But I thought nobody would hire me at that rate. Wrong! But it took a while to get the nerve to post my true hourly rate.

In the meantime, I got really busy with projects, got better at bidding, and increased my skills and systems.

Never gave another thought to the hourly rate posted on my info page. Then I got a gig from a client who wanted to pay my hourly rate for some editing. Now that's awkward. "Um, yeah, about the $28 per hour – it's really $75."

I did the project, but not before going into my profile and updating the hourly rate.

I wondered what would happen. Would the projects suddenly dry up? Would my bidding success rate crash and burn?

Or, would this change somehow make me more appealing to writing clients?

Actually, nothing really happened. No measurable change in the success rate for my bids. Nothing dramatic at all.

But, it's come in very handy after getting gigs. A few times I've had clients ask for more work, on an hourly consulting basis. It's been so nice not to have that awkward moment when the client's shocked by the difference between $28 and $75 per hour. And long term, I think it'll pay off by sort of pre-qualifying my prospects. It's a different client who wants a high-priced writer than the one who just wants to pay the lowest fee possible.

4. **Create excellent bidding templates.**

You don't send them as-is; you customize each one according to the projects' particulars. But you don't want to work so hard every time you place a bid.

Tweak them. Test them.

See which variations get you the most response. You want your bidding process to be as easy as possible. If the site offers a sample template, use it. But re-word it!

This is how you make your first impression on these prospective clients. Proofread it. Read it out loud. Make it perfect.

5. **Get to know the flow of the site.**

Figure out all of this before you start bidding.

You'll find that many of your clients are new to the site, too – you'll make them feel a lot more comfortable if you can lead them through the process. It's not complicated, but it is new to you.

Create a flow chart to help yourself visualize what happens after you're awarded a project. Who does what next? You want to know this process cold before you're in it.

Specifically, on Guru, here's the flow:

(a) Client posts a project.

(b) Writers bid on the project.

(c) Often there's some PDB (Private Discussion Board) email back and forth. The client asks for samples, or has some questions about your proposal or your skills.

There's also a project discussion board, and it's always good to check it if you need more information so you can bid. Usually another writer has already asked your question. If the project details are vague, you can ask for clarification.

(d) The client chooses a writer and awards the project.

(e) You get a notification from Guru, saying you've been awarded the project.

(f) You create the project plan, and the escrow fund request – if you're using the escrow feature (highly recommended, at least with new clients).

(g) You wait for your client to approve the plan and fund the escrow account.

(h) Then you get started. Use the PDB to ask questions, and to submit a draft of the work. I also post the finished project on the PDB and in the Guru Workroom (found in the Project Tracker).

(i) Once your client approves your work, either do an escrow release request or send an invoice.

(j) After clients pay (or release the escrow funds), they can leave feedback for you. They also have the opportunity to endorse you, which is an even higher form of feedback. You can also leave feedback about your clients.

6. Get busy bidding.

You should set a goal for each work day about how many bids you'll place.

Do them first thing when you start working. At first, it could take a while as you get used to the flow of the site. You'll have to sift through the projects to find some you're confident you can do.

It's a good idea to start with about five different types of gigs you'll focus on at first.

For example, you could specialize in keyword articles, website content, editing, ebooks, and press releases. Look for these first and place your bids. Then go back and look at the other projects to see if there's anything interesting.

Keep track of what you've bid on, and what happens with the project.

- Did you get it?

- Did the client award it to someone else?

- Did the client bail on the project without choosing a writer?

- Keep your stats.

7. **Do your best**.

On all of these sites, there's a built-in feedback system. Your feedback is like gold – protect it at all costs. Go the extra mile by beating the deadline, turning in excellent work, and being as courteous as an angel.

You want nothing but perfect ratings. If you get anything less, make sure you pay attention to what went wrong and fix it.

You'll choose better projects with practice, but you need to be prepared for the occasional dog. These are the projects that take longer than you expected, where the client wasn't clear, or where you had to do more revisions than you'd like.

Take it in stride. Be a complete professional. Get your payment and good feedback, and learn from your mistakes.

8. **Ask for endorsements.**

If you've done a good job, and your client is pleased with the results, you've provided something of real value. Now is the time to ask for an endorsement.

Guru has a feedback system, and of course, you want to have all five star results from each job – if not, do whatever it takes so you get perfect feedback next time.

An endorsement trumps a perfect feedback rating. It's a client's way of saying others should seriously consider hiring you.

Often, clients will just automatically endorse you if they're pleased with your work. Some don't know that option exists, though.

Don't be shy – go ahead and ask! Nothing will boost your ranking faster than endorsements.

9. Ask for referrals.

This works for clients you get online and locally. Once you've done a great job for them, ask if they know anyone else who might need your services.

They'll be happy to pass your name along (unless they want to keep you all to themselves, which happens!).

This way, you can really get a lot of mileage out of your marketing. One project could turn into a few projects in the blink of an eye.

Always be sure to thank anyone who gives you a referral. If it's someone local, I always try to send a bottle of wine or some other goodie – or at least a hand-written note. It's a little more complicated with online clients because you don't always have their personal contact information, but be sure to thank them.

10. Follow up with your happy clients.

You do a batch of keyword articles for a client. They're happy. They pay. You go back to looking for work, starting from square one – right?

Wrong!

If someone hires you to write, chances are, you'll be needed again.

Sometimes it's a while between projects. Sometimes they forget they'd really like to work with you again.

But you can solve that easily by staying in touch. Every month or so, if you haven't done anything for a particular client, send a little email.

It doesn't need to be anything fancy or high-pressured. Just a little "Hi – just touching base to see how you're doing with your business. If I can help you with anything, just let me know." That easy.

I'd actually forgotten to do this when I first started.

Shame, shame!

Follow-up is a foundational principle of doing business. You should be in touch with your clients several times a year. How else will they remember how much they liked working with you, what a great job you did, and what an impact the project made on their business?

After I came to my senses, and remembered to do this, I ended up with three clients saying, "Oh yes, I've been meaning to get in touch with you. There's another project. Here it is!" A couple others said they were good for now. Several others didn't answer – and that's okay, too.

Want to go the extra mile?

If you've got contact information for a client, be sure to send a holiday card – especially a Thanksgiving card! They're probably inundated with cards in December – but your Thanksgiving card in November will really make an impact. Plus, that holiday more completely expresses why you'd contact them. You're thankful for their business, and for the opportunity to serve.

Local Clients

What do they say? "A prophet is without honor in his hometown." Right?

Well, it's true of writers, too.

If you wake up one day and start telling people you're a writer, you're going to draw some strange looks and snide remarks. It's like saying you're a rock star or professional athlete!

Most people think "best-selling author" when they hear that someone is a writer.

And I did, too!

Chances are, you never thought "direct mail" or "website content" when you dreamt of becoming a writer. Now that you know this is a great way to make money from your writing talent, you don't give it a second thought. You lump 'commercial writer' right in there with 'author' – same thing once you get right down to it. Someone who gets paid to write.

You've got to keep this perception in mind when you start to build your business.

This is one reason I recommend that people start online on a freelance writing job board – the absence of the laugh factor.

People on these boards don't know whether you've got no feedback because you're truly a newbie, or if you're just new to that board. They don't know that you also wanted to be a ballerina, fireman, and veterinarian before you decided to become a writer.

And frankly, they don't care.

If you can produce some good samples, and you do a good job for them on their projects, you're a writer.

Once you've done a handful of projects for online clients, you can honestly tell people in your world that you're a writer. Just say, "I've started a freelance writing business."

That takes some of the opportunity for smirks away before they have the chance to form.

- You're not claiming to be Ernest Hemingway.

- You're not claiming to be a journalist.

- You're not even claiming to be self-supporting.

You just said you've started a business. The only normal response is, "Oh. That's nice," or some variation. Then, if they follow up with, "Do you get paid?" You can say "Yes, I do – thank you very much."

If you're like me, you've written for a long time before you actually set up shop. You just may not have ever been paid.

The writing bug hit me hard as a kid, in fact. I remember trying to write a novel in seventh grade. I still remember the title: "The Irony of Cold Spaghetti" – it was a coming of age story, full of angst and storm, and my seventh grade teacher really liked it.

Anyway, the writing bug followed me into college and grad school, and I was the proud author of more than a couple of sample papers (you know, the kind the professor keeps for the following year to show the next crop of students how it's done).

I'd also been the go-to gal in the office when anyone had a business letter to write. "How's this sound?" "Did I say this right?" "Would you take a quick look?"

Did any of this translate into being a professional writer?

Nope.

But it was, in fact, writing experience. It just wasn't paid.

So, after having a few projects under my belt, when I began announcing that I was a freelance writer, I was covered.

If someone said, "Huh… I never pegged you for a writer."

Or…

"Really? I had no idea you could write…"

I could (cool as a cucumber) say, "Oh, yeah – I've been writing for years. I just decided to start taking on some new clients." Not bad!

There are tons of people out there who are wannabe writers.

And then there are actual writers.

What separates the two? Writers actually write. You're a writer when you say you are – and when you're actually writing.

Choosing to Have Local Clients or Not

So why would you want local clients anyway? You could easily build an entire freelance writing business with internet-based clients. In fact, I'll estimate that 95% of my clients are people I've never met – or even talked to.

Got to love the internet!

In some ways, it's a lot more efficient to build your business this way.

Some writers crave the connection of meetings and phone calls; others prefer to just get it done with minimal contact. You can go either way with your business.

I recommend a mix of local and remote clients. Where they are is not as important as whether they (and their projects) are ultimately a good fit for what you want to do.

Some benefits of having remote clients:

- **No meetings!**
  This is huge. You can kill a lot of time traveling to a client's office, sitting in the waiting room, then hashing out ideas at the conference table. You might even have to deliver your text in person, sit while they ponder any revisions they want, and return for a check. It's definitely not the most efficient way to do business.

- **No schmoozing!**
  With my online clients, I write a proposal and they either like it or they don't. It has nothing to do with going out for coffee, playing phone tag, making small talk, or whether they liked my suit and shoes.

  It's a lot less personal, but it's also a lot more efficient. Schmoozing is a gambling proposition. I do it – I attend networking luncheons and a referral-swapping group (I'll tell you about that soon.) – but have to admit part of the reason I go is for a little social contact. It's not the fastest path to cash, but it can be fun.

- **You can be a bit more direct.**
  For example, if I've got a new project, I always require a contract and deposit before I write a single word.

  This is a lot easier to manage online. You can tactfully say something like, "As soon as you approve our contract and forward your deposit, we'll be ready to roll."

  If I'm writing for my neighbor across the street, I feel like a heel asking for a contract – and don't feel that great asking for a deposit, either.

  In fact, if something went wrong and I didn't get paid, I'd feel uncomfortable pursuing it – even politely.

  OK, so I'm kind of a wimp about confrontation. My point is, when it's an internet-based client, I've got no qualms about being direct (not rude! just direct). This makes the whole process a lot sleeker.

- **Same thing goes for setting fees.**
  Especially when you're starting out, it can give you a case of the giggles every time you state your hourly rate or project rate out loud.

  This doesn't do much for you professional image when you're face-to-face with a client.

  If you're doing business online, you can crack up, puke in your shoes, and fan yourself with nervous, sweaty palms as you give a project estimate – and your secret is safe.

  They never have to know theirs is the biggest project you've ever bid on, and that you're jumping up and down when you win a bid – or that you turn kind of green when you get a gig and now wonder whether you can actually do the job!

Now, before you go hermit on me (and some days it's tempting), let's take a look at the benefits of working with local clients.

- **It's nice to actually see people now and then.**
  Seriously. It's very easy, once you get busy, to live under a rock.

  Your neighbors will wonder whether you still live there. You'll lose touch with everyone you know on the outside. You might even get scurvy from lack of sunshine.

  Even if you're an introvert by nature, it's good for you to get outside and be with people. We all need a sense of connection and a chance to work on interpersonal skills. You never know who you might help – just by being out and about.

  Life and success are about much more than raking in some dollars – ultimately, success involves helping others. And you can't do that if you won't interact with anyone.

- **It's really easy to get repeat customers and referrals if you have local clients.**
  They get to know you. They see you in the grocery store, at a kid's birthday party, or at church and remember they need a press release. I kid you not!

  I've gotten to the point where I bring my notebook with me everywhere, because guarantee that the time I don't, I'll get a job and have to write the details on a napkin.

- **You might get to try a new skill out on a friend.**
  I have a hair salon nearby, and I'm friends with the owner. We met at a Chamber of Commerce event and hit it off. She and I do networking stuff together, which makes it a lot more fun (love the buddy system – especially when you get cornered by a talkative networker!). But she also hires me to write articles, press releases, her website content, even her service menus and business cards (not a service I usually offer, but if a friend asks… no problem).

  I helped her nail down a killer tagline, and even got to have some fun doing a little bit of design work.

I'll never be competition for a graphic designer, but I think I did okay. She's happy – she got a good deal, and I got to make pretty pictures.

- **It's also really rewarding to see the long-term effect your writing has on another person's business.**
  With online clients, you may or may not ever hear whether your sales letter actually brought in any money. You may never know how their e-book is selling. But with a local client, you'll hear stuff like, "Oh, ever since your press release ran, the phone's been ringing like crazy!" Or, "Hey, Joe – this is the writer I was telling you about. You know what? She wrote the stuff on my website, and now it's actually making money for me."

Local clients can be a good source of regular jobs, but I've found it takes a little more time and effort to get work from them. It's not as direct a process as finding gigs on a job board. Look at the difference:

On a job board, you know that the prospective clients there are there because they want something written.

They know they want it. You know they want it.

Now it's just a matter of showing that you can do the job, and having them give you a shot.

Locally, you don't know what a prospective client's needs are.

- Do they need or want a writer?

- Are they doing all their own writing?

- Do they even have any projects?

- Do they know they could hire out their writing projects?

You're starting from square one.

Just as in any other sales position, you'll have to start with building a relationship. It's really important to do this with local people, because you'll see them in the grocery store! You don't want to be remembered as that freaky writer who was so pushy, obnoxious, and insulting (imagine, implying the text I wrote for my website isn't up to par!).

"Wait a second," you say, "What do you mean by *just as in any other sales position?*"

Yeah, hate to break it to you, but no matter what business you're in (and even if you're just married or have kids or friends), you're in sales.

Get over it.

Sales is truly just matching up what you can do or provide with what someone else wants or needs – an equal trade.

It's really best if you build your online client list first, so you don't go out networking with that "hire me or I'll starve" look in your eyes. It's awfully hard to concentrate on being helpful and friendly when you're desperate. But once you're getting regular work from online sources, it's a great next move to cultivate the field close to home.

So, how do you find these local clients? Here are a handful of ways I've found some of my best clients. Try them out and let me know what works for you.

Chamber of Commerce

The Chamber can be a great source of work, if you do it right. It'll cost you – but you should designate part of your revenue to use for marketing expenses. A membership will probably cost $300 - $500 per year.

On top of that, you'll probably need to pay for networking lunches and breakfasts. So it's not the cheapest way to go. But it can pay for itself with a good project pretty quickly.

A couple of tips:

- **Go to each event with a killer introduction speech.**
  Usually you get about a minute to introduce yourself. If you can't wow them with what you say, you're wasting your time and money.

You just bought yourself one heck of an expensive scrambled egg breakfast.

Make sure your intro stands out as being creative, professional, funny (if possible), and loud enough that everyone hears you. Most people just get up and say the same old stuff, and nobody's really listening. If you can get up and make a positive impression, you'll be amazed who'll come talk to you afterward. Here are two introductions I've used recently that got a good response:

o   At a women's networking luncheon, I went up front with a pillow stuffed under my shirt so I looked pregnant. I said, "Sometimes you've got big news that sort of announces itself." I pulled the pillow out and said, "Other times, maybe you need a press release. I'm Sue LaPointe, owner of Triumph Communications, where choice words help your business succeed."

o   At another luncheon, I went up front, hid my eyes with my arms, and said, "One… two… skip a few… ninety-nine… a hundred! Ready or not, here I come!" Then I looked around, and said, "Hide and seek's a blast when you're seven years old. When you're trying to market your business, it's not so great. If you could use a little help boosting your business' visibility, give me a call." (Then the info about my business.)

The key is to be interesting, without being too weird.

Use props. Shake it up a little. Make sure to bring something fresh each time you go, so that people look forward to your spiel.

There's one networker we see at every event who found a cute, rhyming (ugh!) introductory spiel for her business. It was somewhat catchy the first time we heard it – eight months ago. At this point, we could all recite it. We listen, to be polite, but I know many of us cringe each time she starts up. It beats getting up and being either too quiet for anyone to hear, or just saying your name and what you do (deadly mistakes).

But why settle for just getting it done? Get up there and make an impression!

Lots of people there have no idea what a freelance writer is or does, so you may have to do some educating over the months you're involved. Take it slow and just pick one type of project at a time. Good tasks to mention include: press releases, website content, brochures and marketing materials, and white papers.

- **It's not a meat market.**
  Go to these events (and do go – otherwise, that little plaque you get from the Chamber becomes an expensive dust catcher) with one goal – to meet some nice people.

  Don't go with the goal of making a virtual ticker tape parade of your business cards.

  And don't collect cards like you're going after a complete set. Don't spam these people afterward, either.

  It's better to chat with a few people and really listen to them, than to get with everyone in the room for three seconds each. See whether there's anything you can do to help them with their business or life (recommend a plumber, and accountant, a free advertising venue). Do what you can to be relevant to them. A great book on effective networking is _Love is the Killer App_ by Tim Sanders.

Networking Luncheons

Same kind of idea as going to Chamber of Commerce events, but better, in my experience. In my area, there are a few of these luncheons for businesswomen (sorry guys!) and a couple that anyone can go to.

Some are free – can you believe it? But most run about $15 - $20. They're held once a month, which is nice because it's easy to get too busy networking to actually get any writing done otherwise. Plus, there's no major commitment. You RSVP for the lunches you want to attend rather than committing for an entire year.

Ask around and see whether your area has anything like this. If it doesn't, see if anyone's interested in starting one up with you.

One of the lunches I attend regularly started out with only ten women several years ago. Now it's usually got about 80, and would have more if the restaurant could hold more! Here's a link you can check out: www.powerlunchbunch.com.

A couple of tips:

- **Bring a door prize if you're allowed.**
  Offer a free something writing-related (not a discount coupon!) – it's an easy way to give something that's impressive, useful, and doesn't cost you anything but time.

  A free press release is a great idea.

  Dress it up by making it a gift certificate that's presented beautifully, maybe in a mug filled with candies or attached to a nice bottle of wine. With your prize, include your business card (duh!), and include the value of the prize on its description.

  You'll get extra exposure when your prize is announced, a nice opportunity to sort of audition for a potentially regular client, and worst case scenario – you get something to add to your portfolio.

- **Bring some marketing postcards with you.**
  These are easy to make, and don't cost a ton. I use Vista Print, but not their ready-made templates. Make your own cards, keeping in mind that they serve two purposes – to get your name out there, and to demonstrate your incredible copywriting skills.

  You can get 100 of these postcards for about $30. They're glossy and gorgeous, and beat the pants off of anything you can make at home or at the office supply store.

  I hand them out along with my business card. This way the postcard can explain exactly what I can do to help, and they can keep the business card for reference.

Referral Swap Groups

If you've heard of BNI (Business Networking International), this is what I've got in mind here – maybe minus the price tag! BNI is a fantastic group where you can learn how to present your business creatively, succinctly, and without puking in your shoes when you stand up to speak.

But, it's expensive – really, really expensive.

And while that's not such a problem once you're established, it's not good for writers who are just getting started. That's why a few business owners in my area started a knock-off version of BNI. Our group has the same basics, but nowhere near the expense.

Here's how it works:

- We have only one of any particular type of business involved in the group. For example, we've got one mortgage guy, one plumber, one banker, an organizing lady, one realtor, and one from many other industries.

- We look for referrals for each other during the course of our everyday business.

- We meet weekly for about 30 – 45 minutes to stay in touch, get to know more about what each member does, and keep track of the referrals we've passed to one another.

- At the meeting, we also sort of train one another as a sales team. So, if the air conditioner guy is running a special on ultraviolet air cleaning filters, and they're really good for people who have allergies, he'll tell us about that.

  This makes it a lot easier to be helpful to the people we come in contact with. If I'm chatting with someone at a networking luncheon and she mentions how her son is really suffering this year from allergies, I can say, "Hey, my friend Scott is an A/C guy, and he's got this great filter. You should call him, or I can have him call you with some info."

A couple of tips:

- Come up with some one-stop solutions your group members can remember and promote. For example, you might offer website content for a company's homepage, or a tri-fold brochure, or a press release. Set your price, describe the prospect your deal would be most appealing to, and run with it.

  It might sound like this: "This month, I'm running a press release special. It's perfect for new business owners. For $100, they'll get a one-page press release, submitted to five local and online outlets. I have a simple questionnaire they can complete, which makes it really easy to get the word out about their new business."

- This is definitely a situation where, to quote BNI, "givers gain." The more referrals you're able to find for your group's members, the better they'll do in business. They'll remember this, and be on the lookout for people who need writing done.

Website Developers

This is one of the latest goldmines I've found for writing projects. Typically, business owners hire a firm to make their website for them. They specify colors, graphics, how many pages, and what these pages should cover.

But they rarely provide any content!

These poor techies are left with nothing when it comes time to put words on the site. They ask, beg, and plead with their clients to please send some text. The client usually responds with something like, "Oh, I was hoping you could just write something."

Yikes!

The techies go into panic mode and try to crank out something that reads okay. It's a matter of left-brain, right-brain, I think. They're geniuses when it comes to meta this, and source that – but words are not usually their forte.

The client ends up with a gorgeous site that reads like garbage.

Their prospects take one look and click onto the next business' site. It ends up being a complete waste of money for a company to buy a website and fill it with bad writing. The techies know this, and are more than happy to outsource the content end to freelancers. They can tell their clients that their text will be provided by a professional writer, you get a lot of steady work, and everyone wins!

Take this a step further, and you may never have to market again.

If you live somewhere that has a large population of business owners for whom English is a second language, you can help even more. Many website firms specialize in working with these entrepreneurs, and practically jump for joy when they can provide not only great copy for the site, but copy that's written by a native English speaker. These business owners communicate beautifully in their native language, and sometimes also in spoken English, but this is all lost when they write. It's a very good niche market for freelance writers.

Internet Marketers

You can usually find these folks online – or at conventions and seminars. They're building monetized websites, selling products or information.

One of the primary ways they get traffic is through article marketing.

People read an article online, follow the link in the resource box, and find a whole site devoted to some specific niche – could be about beekeeping, kitchen utensils, narcolepsy, you name it and there's a site about it.

Sometimes these internet marketers can write, and want to spend their time writing – but usually not.

So they're always searching for good content writers. The name of the game for search engine marketing is quality content.

Much of what's out there is absolute garbage – which is good news for freelance writers.

There's no shortage of work! Most of these articles don't even require much in the way of research.

If you build a working relationship with one of these marketers, chances are that they'll keep you very busy. In fact, they become a little territorial about their writers. (Does nice things for your ego!) They appreciate the value of a good writer, and are hesitant even to share your name with a colleague. If they share you, you might get too busy to write for them.

Marketing Tools

Get some great business cards and brochures

This is probably pretty obvious, but do NOT print them on your home printer!

- They look cheap.

- They feel cheap.

- They attract cheap clients!

Not what you want. For about $25 you can get 250 nice, heavy, premium, professionally-made business cards. This is really important, even if you're a one-writer show. You've got to have a sharp-looking card to hand out while you're networking or meeting with a client or prospect.

The brochure is a little less obvious.

If you do it right, you might get gigs doing other business' brochures as well as handling their other writing projects. Take the time to do it right, but don't get bogged down in making it perfect.

Approach it with the mindset of a good copywriter – capturing attention and showing benefits. Nobody wants to read a pricelist – but they do want to know how you can make life easier for them.

It doesn't take much design expertise to create a nice-looking brochure.

Make the design consistent with your business card. Go with a logo or theme you'll use for all of your printed materials. Even a simple graphic of circles and bars will work well. Get them professionally printed on nice glossy paper, and they'll look a lot more expensive than the $1 each you should expect to spend. Just buy about 50 at a time.

They're not something you pass out to everyone you meet – only the ones who ask for more information about what you do.

It's a good idea to come up with some package deals you can offer, and feature them on your brochure. That doesn't work for every writer, but if your list of project possibilities is standardized, you can combine a few to make a nice package.

Just the Right Amount of 'Cute'

(WARNING: This is one of those little matters that can muck up your whole business plan if you let it.)

So, we're not going to go there. I know how much writers like to stew and percolate, looking for just the perfect phrase or name to magically encapsulate their thoughts. It's part of what makes us so 'special' – right?

So hear me clearly: Do NOT get sidetracked by this! Keep building your business!

And once again: I am not giving you 'permission' to halt in your tracks to obsess over this.

Enough warnings? OK. Then we're ready to take a look at this.

What is the name of your business?

Maybe you're just starting out, and haven't even given a thought to this. You're just writing away, taking whatever projects land in your lap. You figure that down the road you'll probably need a business name so you can get a tax entity set up – but it's not really anything anyone would ever see, except your accountant and Uncle Sam.

Or, maybe you've already named your business and you've been building it for a little while. Maybe it's not growing as quickly as you'd like, and you're wondering why.

You might want to give this some thought. There are a couple of ways writers seem to go with the whole naming game.

- One is to use your own name. When your business gets big, you might even add an "and Associates" to the end. Generally, a nice, classy way to go (depending on how kind your parents were in naming you, anyway!). Think of the Big Guys – Bob Bly, Clayton Makepeace, Joe Vitale. Just kind of speaks of quality and effectiveness, huh? The only thing is, chances are that you don't have a whole lot of name recognition starting out. You probably don't have an office space, a phone book listing, or an administrative assistant. In fact, chances are that showering before you get to work is optional because you work from home!

  The trouble is, just naming your company after you doesn't really communicate much at all – except your name. Your prospect is left wondering whether you're a real business, or a guy in bunny slippers.

- The other way writers go is to come up with a company name that's distinct from their own name. For example, mine is Triumph Communications, LLC. My friend Michelle's is Web Friendly Writers. A quick scroll through Google's listing of freelance writing firms shows Zip Writers and Scriptorium – pretty cool names. The names communicate not only what these writers do, but also convey the benefit they bring their clients.

The danger of going with a writing-related name is that you can get too cute. Think about the awful possibilities! A quick look through your phone book at the listings under "Beauty" can give you a glimpse into the horror! "A Cut Above" "Hair Today Gone Tomorrow" "The Hair Barn" "Knot a Barber" "Dye-in to Meet Ya" (OK, I made that one up!)

You don't want to go that route. It is absolutely possible to get too cute for your own good. You don't want to leave your prospects groaning over your bad pun. You want them believing you "get" what they need.

So in a very real way, your company name is nothing short of a sales piece. And what's the number one rule in sales writing? Answer your prospect's question – What's in it for me? Make sure your company name is benefit driven. Come up with something that encapsulates the best thing you provide, what makes you distinctive, what makes life easier for your clients.

Ramp It Up

Once you've got a steady stream of projects coming in, it's time to do some weeding and feeding.

You are in control here.

After you've got this thing in motion, you can steer it exactly where you want it to go. Choose the projects and clients you want to work with – at the fees you want.

I've read that it takes about six months of practicing every day to get good at something, and about a year to become an expert.

It's the same with freelance writing.

You'll find after a while that you enjoy certain projects more than others. Some come easy to you, while some make you pull your hair out. When you're marketing or bidding on projects, you know you're a shoo-in – and your success rate with landing certain projects is overwhelming.

Once this happens, it's time to ramp up your niche.

Unfortunately, your niche may not always be the type of project you love most. I don't know whether anyone really feels fulfilled after writing ten SEO articles about security equipment, but if they're fast and easy for you, SEO might be one of your niches.

It's nice to have a hip-pocket project specialty. These projects make for very streamlined bidding, writing, and submission. Once you've got one niche down pat, start learning about another one (preferably one that pays even better).

For example, many of my earliest projects were content articles. Then I learned how to do SEO articles, and charged a bit more for them. Then I learned how to do e-books.

On the first one, I took a bath (for my Aussie readers not familiar with that particular idiom – it means to take a huge loss) price-wise, but learned enough that I could do it better, faster, and for a much higher fee the next time around.

Then I learned how to write sales letters and web copy, following the same pattern.

In fact, it was kind of funny how the sales letter thing came about.

I bought some templates and studied them. I read Bob Bly's book about creating the perfect sales piece. And I started looking at the sales letters I found online and in my mailbox.

Hmmm – okay, a little cheesy, a little "Ginzu chopping knife"- like, but not that hard to do.

For one e-book I ghostwrote, my client hired a copywriter to do the sales page, and sent me a link. It was kind of weird reading about what I'd written – but I got a lot of tips.

So I placed my first bid on a sales letter - $65, since I hadn't really done one before for real – and got the job.

I used the template only to make sure I was covering all the bases – a call to action, bulleted lists, etc. She loved it! It became a sample.

I bid on my second letter. $100 (figuring what the heck, give it a try).

Got it.

Did it.

They loved it.

Added it to the sample file.

The third letter - $150.

The fourth - $200.

The tenth - $500!

The price could still go up! We could look at setting up a royalties payment structure, too. This was just the coolest experiment in pricing.

Now, I could still be cranking these things out for $65, if I hadn't learned, improved, and raised the price.

The point is, keep going until you really nail certain projects. Get so that you could do them in your sleep. Market yourself as an expert, and have the samples on hand to back up your claim.

For some projects, you're really getting paid for your expertise rather than your work. This is a very nice position to be in – it just takes some sweat getting there.

When You Take a Bath

It will happen from time to time, so don't freak out.

Here's what usually happens:

You see an interesting project – something you're up for learning how to do, say, an e-book.

You bid what seems like a reasonable fee.

You get the project.

You start the project and realize you've bitten off more than you can chew – at that price.

Now what? Do you bail? Do you complain?

Nope.

You chalk it up to learning. You suck it up and do a good job with a big smile on your face. Yes, you're taking a bath on this one.

But think of all the immeasurable value you're getting in return:

- It's like being paid to take a college course.

- You're learning how to do a new task.

- You're learning how to price for next time.

- You're learning which questions you should be sure to ask next time.

- You're learning how to keep your composure, your professional attitude, in the midst of a project you're growing to hate.

- You're also learning what's reasonable to ask of other writers down the road who may help with your overflow work (we'll talk a little about that later).

Treat each project as the wonderful opportunity it is – and learn from everything you do.

Chapter 3 – Legal Mumbo Jumbo

The Importance of the Right Business Entity

Alright. Now that you've got business coming in, you're going to have to make some changes! If you let all this writing come in, in your name, under your Social Security number, you're going to take a beating when tax time comes.

You could have taken care of this before you got your first job, but it's better to do it once you've got a little bit of money coming in.

Do you have any idea how many corporations, partnerships, and LLC's are out there that have never even gotten going?

It's all fun and games naming your business, getting all that paperwork done, and all of that – but until you're actually doing something in the business, it's just a bunch of red tape. Plus, it costs a little something to get all this stuff rolling.

I'm not going to get into too much detail about business entities – there aren't too many other topics much more boring – but I will give you a brief run down of your options.

While it might not be the most interesting topic, the entity you choose for your business will have a big effect on your future – so it's worth learning a little first. The entity determines how you'll do with employment taxes, paperwork, and ultimately, your bottom line.

If you choose unwisely, you can really end up with problems.

Don't panic, though. If you mess this up, you can restructure your business – and even if you do it right, you might need to restructure somewhere down the road as your business grows. But it's a good idea to choose well from the start.

There's no "right entity" for everyone. You've got to weigh your needs and goals to find the one that'll work best for you.

The big differences among each entity type are how they're taxed and how they handle liability. Some types are essentially double taxed, while pass through entities are not.

Business Entities

Sole Proprietor

This can be a single owner or a married couple. It's the simplest entity form. It's a double tax entity, because you get socked with self-employment tax and income tax. You have complete control over the business, but you're also personally liable for all of the business debts and obligations.

C Corp

Another double-tax entity. The earnings are taxed, and then the dividends paid to shareholders are also taxed. These are usually really big companies with many owners. There's a lot of paperwork involved because you have to have shareholder meetings and keep corporate minutes.

Partnerships

Partnerships don't pay taxes at all! But before you do a happy dance, understand that the partners pay the taxes themselves on their personal returns. There are two different types of partnerships – general and limited.

A general partnership requires at least two people to be personally liable for the obligations of the business. Your personal assets are included in the risk, so they can be used to meet any liabilities of the business.

Limited partnerships are a little different. One person is a general partner (risking it all), but the others are responsible only to the extent of their personal investment. The general partner oversees the daily operations of the business.

LLC and S Corp.

Even though it's got the word 'corporation' in it, an LLC really isn't one. It's kind of a cross-breed between a corporation and a partnership.

It brings out the best traits of both because it's less formal and more flexible. Members' assets are separate from the business, so there's no personal liability. But the LLC is also taxed as a partnership, so there's no double taxation.

The S Corp. is a little different. It's actually an election you make when you form an LLC. This election makes it so the business can be taxed as a pass-through entity, so you avoid double taxation.

Employee salaries are subject to employment tax. Any officers who do work on a daily basis have to receive a 'reasonable' salary after the company is profitable, and after it's paid back the officers' initial investment. Shareholder dividends or distributions aren't taxed to the business.

Choosing the Business Entity for Your Needs

So how do you choose? Get a good accountant. Interview them first! As I was starting out, one accountant said not to bother with an LLC – just go as a Sole Proprietor because it wasn't likely I'd make much money anyway.

Hmpf! Next!

Whatever you choose, open a business bank account. You'll probably have to furnish all the paperwork to the bank, and it'll probably cost you a whole afternoon do get it all done. But it's a one-shot time expenditure, and you won't have to mess with it again.

You can learn a lot more about business entities online at <u>Legal Zoom</u>. It's a relatively inexpensive way to get your entity paperwork filed, too. I got my LLC there for about $400, rather than through an attorney's office for about $800.

One more thing!

Most cities and towns require you to have a business license if you're running a business from home – even if you never meet with clients there. You'll want to check with your local government to see what's required where you live. It's not expensive usually, but it could be if you don't do it!

Chapter 4 – All Things Money

How do I charge?

If there's one question freelancers have on their minds, it's this: How much should I charge?

It's a good question.

Charge too little, and you're practically working for free - and you're left wondering whether that 9-5 job might be a better deal after all!

Charge too much, and you might not get any work.

So, what the heck do you say when a prospect asks the dreaded question, "How much would you charge for..."?

Pricing's kind of a big hill to climb. We'll take it in small steps.

The first thing you've got to decide is your hourly rate. Not too many clients will ask about it - although I have a few who have.

Typically, the best situation to run an hourly tab is when you're doing work that's bordering on consulting. For example, I have a client who's always got great ideas buzzing through her head. She'll ask me to spend some time brainstorming how she could market a new site or product. She knows my hourly rate is $100, and I bill her in increments of 15 minutes. We've worked together enough that I bill her monthly, knowing she'll pay.

Even though your hourly rate will work well sometimes, it's almost always better - for everyone - to bill a flat fee.

Why? Think about it.

If you get paid $5 per hour to rake leaves, your employer will wonder whether you're working as quickly as possible, or if you're dogging it.

Right?

But, if you estimate it'll take five hours, and charge a flat fee of $25 to rake the leaves in one yard, they'll feel better - knowing just what to expect.

Now here's the beauty part - what if you become such an efficient leaf-raker that you manage to do that same yard in only three hours?

You've given yourself a raise! Your ingenuity is rewarded. And your employer is still happy - because you kept your end of the deal.

The same idea holds true with your writing.

Why would a client hire you without knowing how much the project will cost in the end? And why would you want your income tied to your time?

A general principle is this: it's always better to get paid by results rather than by time.

But your hourly rate is good to know even when you're charging a flat rate for a project. Especially when you're just starting out, it's a great way to back into your fees for projects you do often.

There's math in them there (pricing) hills!

You might have gotten into writing because you hate math - sure was a plus for me! But you're never really safe from math, no matter what you do.

You can run, but you can't hide.

If there's one thing worse than math, it's math done backwards. But that's just what you'll need to do to get your rates into good shape.

To motivate you to do the math, think about this. If you overcharge, you'll miss a lot of jobs. If you undercharge, you'll hate life! So, it's important.

The first step is determining your hourly rate.

Now, if you've been working in an office for a little while, but not really gotten into a high-paying job, you're probably earning anywhere from $15-$40 per hour. (Of course, it's packaged as a salary, but with a little number crunching, you can figure out your hourly rate.) If you've been in retail or hospitality, the numbers might be a little lower.

So, you might be shocked (and even a little giggly) when you see writers quoting rates of $50 - $200 per hour.

Get over it!

Take a look at other professionals to get the idea.

If you think about attorneys, you'd probably assume the $500/hour guy is better than the $100/hour guy. I know I would - whether it's true or not! So, keep that in mind. You may have to grow into feeling like you're worth $50 an hour.

And that's okay - but do it anyway until you feel worthy.

For writers, words come easy. We don't tend to place a lot of value on things that come easy - we figure anyone could do it, since it's easy. You've got to realize that if you can put words together, you're the exception - not the rule.

You have a talent - and that's valuable.

Now, here's an important thing about pricing. You will make mistakes. And sometimes you'll take a bath. But you'll get better at it if you persevere.

You need a timer. Keep track of how long it takes you to do things:

- How many minutes to write an article?

- How long to do research?

- How long on the phone with clients?

- How fast do you write 500 words? 1000 words?

- How long to proofread?

Warning! Here comes the backwards math part!

Let's take a look at an example. If it takes you 15 minutes to write a 500 word article, and your hourly rate is $60, you need to charge $15 per article to get your hourly rate.

So when you see those article projects listed on job boards, and the employer wants them for $5 each - run! You won't make it up in volume!

Now, what if a client wants a quote for a 100 page e-book?

A general rule is that a page is roughly 500 words (I've seen other writers say it's about 300-350 words, but I go with 500). So, essentially, you'd be looking at 100 pages x $15 = $1,500. Right?

Nope!

There's a big difference between writing 100 one page articles and one 100 page e-book. There's continuity, there's making sure it's not redundant, there's more research, more planning, more EVERYTHING!

I did my first e-book, 100 pages, for $500.

Torture! And a great way to learn about pricing!

So, work with what you can figure out easily, and go from there. Don't be afraid of making mistakes - just learn from them. There's no scarcity of projects.

If you blow your pricing by going too high, you'll have another chance on another project. If you blow it by pricing too low, you'll work like a dog for a while and learn a great lesson for the next time.

As a side note, this is one reason you may want to avoid online job boards that use an open bidding system. This is the kind where you can see what everyone else is bidding for a certain project. The pressure is huge on these boards – you may feel like if you get the gig.

It seems like most of the employers go for the lowest price (not true, but it certainly seems like it). So you'll probably find yourself writing for a lot less don't lower your fee, you'll never than you should be paid. It's tempting, because you figure you can knock out those 500 word articles for $2 each quickly, and at least you'll be working, but it's not the way to go!

How to Make Pricing a Snap

Here's a great way to get some guidance on your fee schedule – team up with other writers! Now the idea here is not to undercut other writers.

"He charges $25 for an article – so I'll charge $23.50!" – not at all what I've got in mind.

In fact, if you do that, you'll find yourself working for pennies pretty quickly, which is definitely not among the reasons you start a writing business.

The goal is to learn the typical fees for projects you do often. Use them as a guide. It's likely you'll be shocked at how little you're charging, compared to other freelance writers.

So how do you get this information? Just ask.

Or, do a little Googling. Some writers post their prices on their sites – and though I don't recommend doing that, it's an easy way to do some sleuthing. Keep a spreadsheet of the prices you find, updating them every time you hear or see what another writer is charging. You'll quickly get a good picture of how your rates compare.

What do you do with the pricing information you find? You use it to make some decisions. Without information like this, you're at the mercy of whatever projects come your way. Armed with info, you know a lot more about fair pricing.

Funny story – the very first freelance writing project I did was an SEO article gig.

I had to use the client's special article-posting template. It counted my words, made sure I'd used the keyword enough times, checked for plagiarism, and made it a snap for them to publish the articles. The gig was this: 600+ word articles, original content, built on 100 different keywords – one per article.

The deadline was tight – and the pay: a whopping $2 per article.

And I was pretty proud to have landed the gig!

I remember telling some relatives about it, when my step-brother started laughing. He said I needed to get an agent, because I was obviously on the losing end of this deal.

I was shocked!

Wait a minute – are you telling me that my words are actually worth something more than $.003 each? It was a turning point!

Raise your prices if they're too low.

You're probably thinking, "My clients will FLIP if I raise prices on them!" And you may be right. It'll take some discernment on your part. You should consider doing incremental increases in some cases.

In other cases, you'd be surprised at how okay they really are with your increases – if you've provided excellent writing services, they'll be happy to pay your new rate because it's easier than finding another writer they like.

Obviously, the easiest situation is to raise your prices for all new clients.

It's also good business to continually evaluate your client base, and weed out the projects and clients that are least profitable for you. I've read somewhere that you should fire the five least profitable client business each year.

The idea is to keep good records and analyze them often.

- What do you expect to do this month?

- How will you do it?

- How's it going?

- How'd you do?

- What can you tweak so you do better next month?

- Where did you waste time?

- What was easy?

- What was most profitable?

Revenue Modeling for the Freelance Writer

Math is everywhere, my friends – and even we who are usually better with letters than numbers have to deal with it (or hire it out, which is a much better choice in my opinion).

The numbers we're looking at involve the prices you've learned how to set. We've got to use them again. But this time it's more exciting, because we'll start connecting the dots, and begin to see how building a successful writing business can bring you one step closer to financial freedom.

So, what's revenue modeling?

It's kind of the happy part of making a budget, rather than the part that makes you feel like you're on a diet. It's all about how much money you have coming in (revenue). The modeling part speaks to the fact that you're creating a model.

*hen you're just starting, it'll feel a

to have to haul out the calculator,

,onderful things for your business. It helps
toward the most profitable writing projects. It
now closer you're coming to your goals. And it helps you
your business in an orderly way rather than running in every
direction at once, chasing after dollars like a lion after the slowest
antelope in the pack.

OK, so if you're not quivering in a corner, let's start.

You'll need your price list, a spreadsheet, and your monthly income goal.
Start with your goal. We'll use $5,000 per month as an example (and one
that's very attainable – even modest).

So how do you create that $5,000 in revenue? Well, there are many ways
to meet that goal: one $5,000 e-book, two $2,500 websites, ten $500 sales
letters, or 200 $25 keyword articles, just for a few examples. The
combinations and possibilities are endless.

Think about what's been the most profitable and frequent project for
you. If you've never done an e-book, that's probably not the best plan. If
you're moonlighting, cranking out 200 articles per month might be a little
much. Work out the combination of projects that works best for you.

Here's where the guess-work comes in. Unless you've already produced
$5,000 per month, it's hard to tell which combination of projects you're
most likely to hit your target with.

But that's okay. Just come up with something.

Say you decide to go with 200 $25 articles. The next step is to look at
where they'll come from. Do you have a client who needs that many? Are
you bidding on a freelancers job board? Are you doing some networking?

Being that 200 is a nice, round number, you can see the next step coming - pacing your activity. You need to crank out 50 articles each week for four weeks. This means 10 per day (if you work 5 days a week). If each article takes 20 minutes, you're looking at just over 3 hours of solid writing per day.

You should build in time for marketing, planning, paperwork, and taking care of yourself. All of that can easily be done in another 3 hours. So, you're up to 6 hours of work per day. Not bad!

Next, you've got to keep track of how you're doing throughout the month. Really concentrate on bidding, trying to hit your goal – especially early in the month. If you can line up all your work early on, you've got the rest of the month to focus on doing it. It can help if you mentally bump your deadline up by a week or so.

So, if you're aiming for $5,000 each month, try to get that much work scheduled by the third week. Sure beats scrounging for a few more gigs during the last two days of the month, trying to hit your goal.

How Do I Make Sure They Pay?

Kind of important, isn't it? After all, it's kind of the whole point of running a business.

Online clients through a job board

When you get a gig with a new client through Guru (and I'm assuming the other freelance boards have a similar provision in place), use the escrow fund. It's there to protect you and the client.

You send a funding request.

The client deposits money into the escrow account.

Guru holds it.

You finish the work.

The client approves the work.

You request an escrow fund release.

The client hits a button, and you've got money!

If there's a dispute, the money's there. Guru will help arbitrate the case so that everyone leaves happy. I have NEVER had to do this, but like knowing it's there – just in case.

If you don't use the escrow option, Guru can't do a thing to help you chase your money.

Always use the escrow option when you're dealing with a new client. After a while you'll build a relationship together, and it's fine to just send an invoice then.

Invoicing costs less, too – the escrow option adds a bit to the project fee (which is deducted from your pay). Some clients you'll work with so often that they'll just ask for a Paypal invoice – even less deducted from your pay!

Other online clients

If you didn't find them through Guru, you can still use the Guru escrow function. I've never done it, though. Instead, I ask for a deposit of ¼ - ½ of the project fee, depending on how big the project is.

For a large project, I let them pay in four installments. For a smaller one, I ask for half.

There's a little risk, but not much. I've been stiffed only three times, and every single time, it's been because I bypassed the escrow or deposit system.

Part of the anti-stiffing protection is being selective about your client list, and setting your prices high enough to weed out the tire-kicking thieves who'll take your work and run. You can always go to Small Claims Court, but who's got the time? Try to prevent the problem from the start. Use a standard contract, and get a deposit.

Either Way

No matter where you got your client, make sure to keep every single piece of correspondence. Set up a folder in your email program for the client so all you have to do is move or copy.

If it's a local client, and you're not corresponding via email, you're crazy! (kind of kidding… a little)

Email is the most efficient way to go back and forth, and you've got any specs and particulars right in front of you rather than having to dig back through your notes.

Also, make sure that every payment you receive comes through correctly in regards to your entity.

For example, if a client sends me a check made out to me personally, I send it back and remind them it needs to be made out to my LLC.

Of course, you should specify this in your invoice or purchase order. Sometimes they just forget. Your CPA will thank you for getting it done right.

Fill Your Writing Calendar the Easy Way

Know that saying about how it costs a lot more to get a new client than it does to keep current clients happy? It's true, of course. And it's a great reason to build long-term writing relationships with your clients.

It doesn't always work out.

Sometimes the project's a one-shot deal. Sometimes you'll decide you don't want to work with this client again (a luxury you'll enjoy pretty quickly as you begin building your business).

But when you can get an ongoing arrangement, it's a great thing.

The key to landing a regular gig with your favorite clients is to suggest developing an editorial calendar. It's a huge help to them, especially if they're internet marketers.

Why?

One great way internet marketers drive traffic to their sites is by publishing articles and press releases with links back to the site. By publishing one of each, or even one of either, every month, they'll enjoy a dramatic increase in traffic, backlinks, and eventually, page rank.

But coming up with topics and remembering to hire a writer month after month is kind of a pain for most clients. Just like any other business owner, internet marketers yearn for someone to take care of it for them. They'd rather just approve the article, pay your invoice, and not have to worry about the details.

You can offer a valuable service to your clients by helping them develop an editorial calendar. Provide them with a list of great reasons to send out press releases. They might have some newsworthy events planned already, or your list might provide even more value as it spurs their creativity.

Here's a list I send to my clients to spark their imaginations:

The 100 Best Times to Publish a Press Release

Introductions

(Brand new businesses, organizations, products, and services)

1. Starting a new business

2. Introducing a new product or service

3. Introducing a unique strategy or approach

4. Launching a website

5. Announcing a new book or e-book you wrote

6. Listing new publications

7. Introducing unusual products or services that you offer

8. Introducing new trademarks

Updates

(Name changes, product changes, and other announcements)

9. Highlighting new uses for your products or services

10. Announcing the opening of new branch or satellite offices

11. Giving notice about changes to the company or product name or branding

12. Informing about the moving, expanding or renovation of your business

13. Announcing the restructuring of your business or its business model

14. Announcing the forming of a new strategic partnership or alliance

15. Announcing a major joint venture

16. Publicizing changes in pricing, especially reductions

17. Announcing the change of ownership of a company

18. Highlighting your redesigned website

19. Announcing new products or services on your web site

20. Informing about product upgrades or changes

21. Announcing that you've developed a new technology in your industry

22. Announcing the passage of an important company resolution

Marketing Efforts

23. Offering an article series for publication

24. Announcing availability to speak on particular subjects of interest

25. Announcing a public appearance on television, radio or in person

26. Offering free information and online newsletters

27. Announcing the results of applicable research, surveys, studies or reports

28. Sponsoring a workshop, seminar or trade show

29. Making public statements on future business trends or conditions

30. Announcing a free chat room class you're teaching

31. Giving away online products or services

32. Starting an online business association or club

33. A famous person is endorsing your business

34. An expert or celebrity is speaking in your chat room

35. Hosting a fundraising event at your web site

36. Having a contest or sweepstakes at your site

37. Participating in major sponsorships online

38. Attending a trade show or exhibition

39. Making speeches and offering reprints on your website

40. Holding a competition or contest

41. Hosting a celebrity visit

42. Interviewing or meeting with a celebrity

43. Publishing projections and forecasts

44. Forming committees, or announcing membership for committees

45. Making a donation to charity

46. Organizing or participating in a charity event

47. Having a tie-in with a national holiday, a birthday or anniversary

48. Co-hosting an event with the media

49. Offering first person stories about people using your product or services

50. Sending a letter to the editor

51. Giving directions about applying for internships with your company

52. Giving directions about applying for scholarships offered by your company

53. Announcing a fact finding trip and reporting your findings

54. Making hand-outs available

Staff News

55. Announcing new training programs for employees

56. Reporting qualifications received by employees

57. Announcing staff promotions

58. Recognizing long-term employees and retirees

59. Announcing appointments

60. Reporting the results of an election

Customer News

61. Obtaining a new, significant customer

62. Setting up a customer advisory group

63. Announcing new contracts that you've won, clients you've obtained, etc.

64. Publishing your customers' success stories and testimonials

65. Recognizing awards given to customers

Community Activities

66. Participating in a philanthropic event

67. Contributing to the community

68. Volunteering time to help the community

69. Fund-raising or other events for the local community

70. Sponsoring local programs or events

71. Offering internships with local schools

72. Offering scholarships for local students

73. Organizing a tour of your business for local residents

74. Staging a debate

75. Sponsoring a special event

76. Issuing a commendation

77. Issuing a protest

78. Inspecting or reporting on a project

79. Writing a letter

80. Releasing a letter you've received

81. Appearing before a public body concerning a local issue

82. Scheduling a speaking engagement at the local library... for free

83. Creating an award to honor individuals in the community

Inspired By News & Current Events

84. Issuing a statement of position regarding a local, regional, or national issue

85. Adapting a national survey or report for local use

86. Taking part in a controversy

87. Commenting on a controversy

88. Reporting on a public project and offering insight to the problem

Accomplishments

(Awards, certifications, anniversaries, media coverage)

89. Winning an award

90. Announcing an appointment

91. Earning recognition of the company, product, or executives by a publication

92. Announcing that you've reached a major milestone

93. Establishing a unique vendor agreement

94. Meeting some kind of unusual challenge or rising above adversity

95. Announcing that an individual in your business has been named to serve in a leadership position in a community, professional or charitable organization

96. Announcing certification of your organization

97. Announcing memberships in associations

98. Observing company anniversaries

99. Recognizing awards won by employees, and

Finally, #100 - Announcing successful litigation

You can also suggest a series of articles reviewing or promoting their product or service. They may want a different product highlighted each month – or for different holidays or seasons.

You'll become an expert on their industry, which makes you even more valuable. And all the while, your writing services become valuable, then invaluable. And that, my friends, translates into regular, and well-paid work.

Chapter 5 – The Real Scoop on Writing at Home

"Do you have what it takes to work at home?"

How many times have you read articles with that title?

Seems like a no-brainer to me! After all, who would really prefer getting up when it's still dark, shoving kids out the door, commuting, dealing with bossy bosses and dysfunctional co-workers, eating an unsatisfying lunch, working late, stressing about picking up the kids, and then coming home to a home you rarely get to see?

Well, apparently, some people do!

But since you're reading this, you're obviously looking for a way to make it work either now, or sometime soon.

Some writers are able to just jump right in full-time, and others decide to ease into the freelance writer lifestyle. It takes a bit of an adjustment, but once you do it, you'll probably join the ranks of the unemployable.

You'll be so hooked on working for yourself from home (or wherever else you happen to go) that the idea of cubicle life seems like a faint memory.

One assumption we've got to make first, though. Any kind of working from home deal is dependent on this.

You MUST be a self-motivated person.

If you're waiting around for someone else to tell you what you must do, you're sunk. If you can't motivate yourself to work rather than watching Oprah (although I love her generosity – wouldn't it be great to give cars away?!) and cartoons, you're sunk.

Not that you'll be perfect at this right off the bat.

Some of this requires discipline, and that's a learned character trait. But you've got to have that basic drive to have any chance of reaching your goals. Otherwise, you've got a hobby, my friend.

The Secret of Running a Home Business… Is to Run It Like a Business

Some tips I've learned along the way.

- **Set office hours.**
  You're the boss, so you're still the master of your time, but by setting some simple guidelines for yourself, you'll know when it's time to work and when it's time to not work.

  Sounds silly, but it's actually much harder to learn to stop working than to keep yourself on task during the day. Decide how many hours a week you want to work. Then block them out on your calendar. Those are now your work hours. If you need to schedule an appointment during that time, go ahead – but know that you're cutting into your work time.

- **Work while you're "at work" and stop when you're not.**
  Ugh. OK, this one's still dogging me sometimes. Not so much the first part, but the second one.

  It's awfully tempting to get back on the computer at all kinds of odd hours, even after my allotted time is up. Why? Because there's always more that can be done. And because the "office" isn't somewhere I have to drive to get to, it's always right there waiting for me. We'll look at this a little more in a bit.

- **Think of IBM. (Or Apple, I guess!)**
  While it's work time, do not do anything you can't imagine the CEO of a big corporation doing in his or her office. This means no laundry, no watching TV, no washing dishes while you're on the phone, no housecleaning, no checking email over and over (ouch!), no laying around in jammies (well, bunny slippers are okay).

  If you imagine the CEO doing it, and it makes you giggle, you're busted. If it's so funny that the CEO is doing it on work time, why isn't it funny that you'd do it, too?

  You are running a business. Sure, you're not wearing a tie or panty hose most days. You're not wheeling around inside a cubby, standing at the water cooler, shuffling your in-box papers – but you are in business. Take it seriously.

- **Back to the bunny slippers.**
  We all joke about writing in our jammies, but only because it's so tempting. It's fine on days you're not feeling great, but not for your every day working day.

  Do yourself a favor every day and get showered, dressed, made up, shaved, whatever you'd normally do for a regular job. This includes shoes. If you hate shoes, you'll balk at this. But if you're willing to do an experiment, give it a try.

  Try working with your shoes on all day for a while and see what happens to your productivity.

So, how much time does it take to do this?

Trick question!

Obviously, there's no set answer here. That's the beauty of it.

You can work an hour a day, or eight, ten, or eighteen. It all depends on what you want to do, and how quickly you want to do it. It also depends on whether you've got children at home, whether you're working at another job, and whether you're in the middle of a big project with a tight deadline.

It is absolutely realistic to expect to get yourself so booked with projects that you could work day and night. I don't recommend doing that, because life starts to stink that way. But my point is that there's no shortage of writing projects you can get and do.

The important thing to remember is that you're in charge of how much you work.

How to Get More Writing Done in Less Time

Freelance writing is one of those businesses where you could work night and day – every day – and still not be "done".

There's always another project bid to place, a little more tweaking you could do, a bit more polishing and proofing.

Will all this perfecting improve your final text? Probably.

Will it drive you crazy? Definitely.

Is it necessary? No way.

What's at stake?

Several "small" things like: your sanity, your family, your social life, your physical wellbeing, and ultimately, your ability to stick with the business you're creating. It's in your best interest to get the big, ugly monster of inefficiency under control when your business is in its infancy – and not to wait until it's got its foot on your throat.

Let's take a look at some ways to become more efficient and effective in your writing.

- **Do one thing at a time.**
  Read that one again, because most likely you've heard the opposite advice throughout your school and working years. We're told to become masters of 'efficiency' by doing more than one

thing at all times. Brush your teeth while you dry your hair. Check email while you're on the phone. And here's the biggie for freelancers who work from home – pop in a load of laundry while you're working.

If you've ever found yourself walking into a room and wondering why you went there, you've experience the downside of multitasking.

You're in action, but you're not really accomplishing anything. You'll spend more time retracing your steps, trying to remember where you left off.

If you'll just focus on the task in front of you, and do it until you're done, you'll be amazed by the jump in your productivity. Now, this doesn't mean that you've got to work on a task until *it's* done – just until you're done. Give yourself a deadline, then set a timer and get to work. When the dinger dings, you're done for this session.

C'mon, it'll be fun – a little game of beat the timer!

Seriously, though – remember back in school when you had a paper due the next morning, and you just couldn't get it to come together? When you finally buckled down and cranked it out, it came out great – and you got an A (I hope!). There's a beauty to deadlines – it forces efficiency and effectiveness. I've gone through a few egg timers – the kids usually make off with them, or the dog knocks it across the room, or they just give up the ghost on me – but they're cheap, and an incredibly valuable tool for getting the job done.

- **Sleep on it**

It sounds really corny, but I like to let new projects percolate for a day if possible. Then all of a sudden, there you are – in the shower, driving somewhere, or just waking up – and POW! You've got it nailed.

This is especially powerful for writing sales copy. You can stew and fuss, trying to find the perfect headline for your sales piece, and get nowhere. It works great for feature articles, children's books, and taglines, too. Anything that really needs a burst of inspiration.

When I was at a seminar, I learned a great tool for stimulating creativity. It's something that Thomas Edison is rumored to have used, and he did okay in the creativity department, don't you think?

The exercise is this:

Sit in a chair with your feet flat on the floor.
Hold your keys in your hand, and put your hands on your knees, palms up.
Close your eyes.
Focus on every body part, one at a time, from your feet upward to your scalp, and imagine them melting into the floor.
Breathe deeply the whole time, and keep your thoughts on the melting, not on your to-do list.
Once you've reached your scalp, imagine yourself in a peaceful place – the beach, by a creek in the mountains, wherever you feel most still. For most people, this place involves water, so I use the beach.
Really feel yourself being there.
Pay attention to what you see, hear, smell, feel, and taste there.
After a few moments, start coming back by imagining your body solidifying again – from the feet up to the scalp. The whole thing should take about 10 – 15 minutes.

Think you'll fall asleep if you sit still that long? That's why you're holding the keys! If you nod off, you'll drop them and the clattering sound will wake you up!

What If You've Got Children?

This is where the good, the bad, and the ugly comes out.

The good first.

Your kids can learn a lot by watching how you run your writing business. They see work, entrepreneurialism, and goals in action. You can talk about projects you're doing, how you solved a problem, interesting things you learned about.

Occasionally, you might even get some sort of neat "toy" to show and share.

I've gotten sample products from a couple of clients because they knew I'd be able to write better copy if I had their widget in hand. And a couple of times, it's been something my kids thought was pretty cool.

Your kids might even learn a lot if they hear you on a business phone call. It's a glimpse of Mom or Dad in a different context. It's kind of like how cool it is when you visit your kids at school. You see them in action, doing their thing.

You also have a great opportunity to teach them to build a business of their own someday. It might not be as a freelance writer, but you never know. As your kids get older, you can use your own business as a teaching tool for them.

One of my goals is to do this so that our kids will know how to make money (a cash machine) at will. This way, when they go to college, they'll be able to study whatever interests them, rather than choosing a major based on what 9 – 5 job they can get when they graduate.

It's the classic case of teaching a man to fish rather than giving him a fish sandwich. You can show by example how to run and build a business.

You can also involve your kids directly in your business if they're old enough. I've had some projects that involved interviewing children. Other times I ghostwrote children's books, and needed a test audience. If you talk to your accountant, you'll find some possible tax benefits available by hiring your children.

The bad.

Parents always feel guilty, so it should be no surprise that you'll probably have a whole new kind of guilt once you start your business at home.

There will be times you've got to meet a deadline, and it'll be hard to go out and play Frisbee. Other times, you'll have to take a business call –

and you can bet that's when your child will HAVE to ask you something. Your kids may complain that you're "always" on the computer.

So you do have to watch it.

It's tempting to just keep working, but you've got to have boundaries. If you're truly focused during your office hours, you're getting enough done. You don't have to let work bleed over into your family time.

If you do, you're blowing it on a few fronts.
(By the way, I'm writing this to me just as much as to you!)

Your kids will get warped ideas about work, about how hard or easy it is to make money, about their value relative to your job, about how you value them and time with them, and about what it's like to be an adult. So be a good example!

One way that works well is to work efficiently, effectively, and with great focus during the hours they're in school (if they're that age). Then put it all away when they get home. If you need to get back to "the office" afterward, wait until they're in bed. This way, they never really see you on the computer. You're getting some enforced down-time and balance in your life.

Kids are great like that – if you'll let them, they'll help you live a much healthier life.

Another trick is to get a "fake" phone number. There are several websites where you can sign up for an inexpensive local phone number that goes right to voicemail. You get an email to notify you whenever you get a message. I use that number on all of my marketing materials.

It helps screen out undesirable calls and also ensures that clients get a professional greeting whenever they call.

This is great because there are just some times when I can't answer the phone – it's either too noisy, we're doing something together, or the dog is barking.

There's also no chance of one of my children answering the phone this way. That phone number can do a lot to protect your professional image!

The ugly.

We're not going to dwell long here.

To keep it short, just be on the lookout for using your business as a "chicken exit." You know, like at an amusement park, when you're standing in line for a roller coaster? When you finally get up to the front of the line, there's this little gate off to the side. It's called the chicken exit.

Family life can be challenging. Parenting is absolutely not for the faint of heart.

There are times when it's a LOT easier to just work than to do what you should do with your family. Workaholism can be very destructive, and you've got to keep an eye out for it. Your family is your family, and your kids won't be children very long. Enjoy them.

How to Take Time Off – Without Killing Your Business

It hits right about the same time every year – that irresistible urge to get away.

The kids are out of school. The weather's getting hot (and humid, at least here). There's the beach, the pool, the family vacation, a writing retreat – all sorts of places to go and things to do.

And they're all calling you to join in.

But now you've got this thriving writing business. You built it. It needs you. And you can't very well just walk away for a week.

Or can you?

Ask the butcher, the baker, and the candlestick maker (or even just your local networking friends), and you'll hear the same refrain: "I can't take time off, because if I'm not working, I'm not getting paid."

So, sadly, they don't – except maybe once a year.

In my experience, even the worst "jobs" I've held gave more than one week off per year! No way, no how is a business I build with my own two hands going to be worse than that.

That brings us to the real sticking point.

Unless we're getting paid royalties, affiliate commissions, sales from an e-book, or other passive writing income, we don't get paid unless we work.

How can you structure your writing business so you can take time off, without having to start from square one again when you get back? Are you doomed to spending your "vacations" staring at your computer screen, cranking out articles, press releases, sales letters, and e-books?

It takes some planning ahead, and nerves of steel (at least the first time), but it's absolutely manageable – and oddly enough, you might be surprised to find a jump in your business (and fees) when you do this.

As your vacation time gets closer, continue bidding on jobs and doing your usual marketing activities. However, when you discuss the timeframe for the project, make it clear that you are unavailable to start until a certain date (a day or two after you get back).

It might sound something like, "If you're interested in moving forward with your project, I can schedule it to start as early as (date)." Sometimes they need it now (or yesterday!), and it won't work out. But often as not, your clients will be fine with it, understanding that you are an in-demand writer.

Can you see the added-in bonus here?

If you continue this pattern of booking yourself ahead, only taking rush jobs if you've truly got some extra availability, what would happen to your business?

Think "Bob Bly" – or one of the other big guys. My guess is that people wait a while to get on his schedule. They're happy to wait, because at least they're ON the waiting list, and they know they're going to get some spectacular writing for their trouble.

If Bob were immediately available, you'd assume something went terribly wrong! Why should it be any different in your business?

Project Management – Otherwise Known as Spinning Plates

When you're just starting as a writer (that's some of you – for others it's just a distant memory), your project management needs are pretty simple. After all, how complicated can it be to write a single 500 word article, submit it, invoice it, and get paid? Frankly, this is the least of your worries at this point. It's like keeping up with dishwashing – and owning only one plate.

But, if you're diligent and effective in seeking work (warning – shameless plug for my book on this goes here) it won't take long before you've got more plates than Bridezilla at Tiffany's. You'll begin to feel like a circus performer, deftly spinning plates high in the air on nothing but a skinny stick. The crowd (your clients) is going wild. You're getting applause (or in our case, paychecks), hoots, and hollers (feedback, referrals, and endorsements). It's thrilling, exciting, and a little scary all at once.

How long can you keep it up? What if you drop a plate? What if one just kind of gets away from you? Without a good system of project management, it won't be long before you start to feel like you're running downhill with a boulder chasing you.

And that's not much fun. Especially if you do drop the ball, er, plate.

Now before you head out to Staples to get the latest and greatest in project management software, let me share a very simple system. You can take your pick. Then, if you're still bent on dropping a small fortune for a fancy system, knock yourself out – and let me know how it's working for you.

I was that chick running down the hill followed by a boulder last year. My writing business had gone from nothing to thriving in less than six month's time. And then it went into overdrive when I expanded it to include a team. Project management worries were waking me up at night. So, I hired a pro. And I'm going to share with you, for the low, low price of nothing, what she taught me.

Take that trip to Staples, or Barnes & Noble, Borders – wherever you can find a good selection of journals. Get one that's meets these requirements: wire bound, hard cover, lined sheets. Also pick up a pack of sticky notes – get the largest size that will fit in your journal. While you're there, get one of those big alligator clippie things (I'm sure they have a name??).

This is your ONE notebook for the next few months. It shall never leave your side. You will not write anything anywhere else – that means no stickies stuck to your computer, no legal pads, no miscellaneous scraps of paper. Anything you need to write, you write in the notebook.

Each week, you will date pages for that week only. On each day's page, you will write any appointments, deadlines, or obligations. You will write whatever you need to get done that day. When you do it, you cross it off. If you don't do it, you will write it on the next day.

Other random things you'll write in this ONE notebook: If you talk with a client and need to take notes, go to a blank page just past the current week and do it there. If you write your goals out daily or weekly (please tell me you're doing this!), you can do it on the back of each day's page. If you do a devotional, Bible Study, or something like that, and need to take notes, go to another blank page just past the current week. Write the phone numbers of people you call, so you've got them recorded. Record your mileage and where you went.

Now, you've been eyeballing those sticky notes, haven't you? Here's where they come in. On one sticky, write these headings: Project, Status. If you work with a team of writers, you'll also want to include a heading called Writer. Each time you get a new project, you'll fill out the particulars here. Include a brief description of the project – client name, word count, due date, price. For the Writer column, record who's working on it, when is it due back to you, and what you are paying. For the Status column, note when you submitted the work, when you invoiced it, and when you were paid.

Clip the sticky note to the back inside cover of the notebook. Flip through these stickies every day to make sure you're on top of all your projects. As projects on the stickies are complete (all the way through getting paid), chuck the sticky. When your ONE notebook gets filled, put it away. You may never need your notes, but if you do, you've got them.

I've been using my "ONE notebook" system for nearly a year now, and it has never failed me. You can't beat the price; it's never been affected by a power outage or computer glitch; and I've also been able to share it with people in other fields – and it works for them, too.

Got Some Down Time? Milk It!

Once you get rolling with your freelance writing business, down times will probably become few and far between. In fact, at this point, if I want some down time, it's got to be scheduled. A wonderful problem, right? Absolutely! This means the machine is functioning properly. Pull the handle, and out pops a bunch of projects. If you're not there yet, never fear – if you persist, it will happen.

What's up with this phenomenon? Why, when the butcher, the baker, and the candlestick maker are moping around complaining that it's costing them money to even open the shop these days, are freelance writers humming along as if nothing were going on in the economy?

I'm no economist, so I'll take a stab at a few quick reasons – and if you're still questioning whether there's money to be made as a freelance writer, listen up!

1. Smart business owners don't ease up on their marketing during a downturn. They do the opposite. They ramp it up, getting the word out more powerfully and creatively than ever before. They try new venues they've never even considered. And guess who they need to hire to help them? Bingo!

2. Freelance writers aren't constrained by the local economy. Somewhere in the world, people are spending – might not be in your city, or even your country, so you need a way to find them. And guess what? There's something about exchange rates, too, that seems to give us a little advantage. My international clients rarely balk at the same fees that sometimes make the domestic ones wince. Ka-ching!

3. Little or no overhead. From the writer's point of view, gas prices become practically irrelevant – at least as far as operating expenses go. Unless you've got office space somewhere (and we all crave that from time to time!), you don't have to pay rent. We don't even pay much for office equipment and supplies. If you've

got a computer and internet access, you're pretty well set. I don't even remember the last time I had to print something out!

So anyway, what if you DO happen to have some unwanted "unscheduled downtime" in your calendar? What's the best way to use it to keep your business moving forward?

Here are eight projects I'd recommend. They'll keep you out of trouble, improve your skills and knowledge, and position you to hit the ground running when you fill your calendar again.

1. **Examine and update your portfolio.**
   What are you showing your prospects? If your samples are growing mold, it's time to freshen up. Evaluate each piece, scanning your memory and your files to see whether you've got another sample that's even better. Are your pieces in Word? No, no, no! PDF those babies – it looks more professional and it makes them harder to be "borrowed" without your knowledge.

2. **Bid on jobs.**
   "Oh no, here she goes again," you're saying. Yes, the debate rages on about the writing job boards (Guru, Elance, etc.). If you're a big-time copywriter, you're probably not going to look there for work. But, then again, you're probably not looking *anywhere* for work at that point – it's coming to you. Until then, you can't beat developing a reliable, systematic way of getting projects – and these sites are great for that. (Hint: you'll be hearing more about this soon!)

3. **Study and practice copywriting.**
   Mastering copywriting is the absolute best way I know of doubling or tripling your hourly rate. In fact, at my recent physical, I was chatting about it with my physician (yeah, he's that thorough!). When I told him what I'm charging these days for a 5-7 page sales letter, his jaw dropped. Ha! And writers don't have to be "on call" either!

4. **Create your own products.**
   Long about the second e-book you write for a client, it'll hit you: Hey! I could do this for myself and build an info marketing empire! 'Nuff said.

5. **Visit forums.**

This one I'm a little nervous about suggesting. There are some forums that are a double-edged sword. You can get an insider's perspective on what clients are looking for; you can even find clients – but you can also shoot an entire day, running down meandering rabbit trails. So set a timer, and head off to a site like www.warriorforum.com or www.wahm.com.

6. **Start a blog.**

Not one that's just all about your life. Start one on something you're passionate about. Something you may eventually want to write a book about is even better. I recommend Blogger (for reasons I'll get into in the "other" newsletter eventually). If you start now, you'll learn the ins and outs of blogging. You can also qualify to blog for pay after a while.

7. **Read.**

Read anything. Reading sparks creativity, boosts your vocabulary and fluidity, and basically oils the gears in your mind.

8. **Learn how to build websites.**

This is a skill every freelance writer should pick up. It's not that hard (heck, if I can do it, anyone can do it!), and it will come in very handy, very soon.

There are lots of programs out there, I'm sure. The one I use is XSite Pro. What I like about it is that it's very intuitive. It works like lots of other programs I've used. You don't have to know html at all, either, because it's a WYSIWYG deal. If you can send an email, you can build a site.

HOWEVER, you really, really should do the tutorial before you get rolling. Even if you think you don't need to. It only takes about an hour, and you're building a real site as you learn.

Why is this a good use of your downtime?

Lots of reasons:

1. It's another service you can offer your clients. It's especially attractive to internet marketers who are just starting out. If you can build the site AND write the content, you're the hero!

2. It's not hard – it just takes some time to learn. And if you're swamped with other projects, chances are that you're not going to want to take the time to learn website building.

3. There will come a time when it dawns on you, "Hey! I could use my writing skills for my own benefit!" If you get into information marketing, you can produce your own products, press releases, articles, and sales copy. You won't want to pay someone else hundreds or thousands of dollars to build a site for you. If you learn how to build sites for yourself, it's the proverbial "teach a man to fish" deal – you'll be able to create all kinds of income streams.

Chapter 6 – Technical Stuff

Now we'll move onto some technical questions. These can help you shave a bit off of your learning curve, and help you project a competent image.

Some of these I learned the hard way, so if I can help you avoid looking like an idiot, I'm glad to oblige!

How do I write about something I know nothing about?

This will happen.

Most of the time, probably.

I've written on topics you wouldn't even believe, and my clients have always been happy. You can easily write about topics that don't interest you, or that you don't know anything about – if you know how to do good, quick research.

Here's where your articles come full-circle. Chances are, your client wants articles that a layperson will understand. Otherwise, you're looking at a technical writing gig, and I don't have much to say about those.

This means you actually have an advantage over someone who's inside that particular field or business, because you can write it in simple, easy-to-understand words. If you do a quick search in a couple of article directories, you'll find oodles of articles on every topic under the sun. And generally, they're all written in plain language, too.

Now, many unscrupulous "writers" out there will simply copy, paste, and bill. WE DO NOT DO THAT!! However, if you think about it, there are really very, very few truly original ideas out there.

Think about it – on the topic of losing weight, they all kind of go with two main ideas: eat less and move more.

You could easily get those ideas from another person's article, then write an entirely original article in your own words.

So, if you've got to write an article on digital security devices embedded in stuffed animals (yes, I've had that one!), you can go looking for an article on that topic, read it, and use the information you've learned to write an entirely new article. By the way, your article will most likely end up in the same directory where you found your source material! In a way, all this info comes full-circle.

You do not need to be a subject matter expert (SME) on anything in order to write about it, unless you're on a tech writing gig – and even then maybe not. If you run into a client who wants you to write articles on their brand-new, patent-pending, Nobel Prize winning technology or idea, politely decline.

You can kill a lot of time doing in-depth research. That's really not the ideal gig if you're building a business. It's fine for magazine writers and journalists, but you don't have time to do exhaustive research, reconnaissance, or investigative reporting.

How Do I Handle Interviewing Someone?

This doesn't happen too often, actually. And there will be some trial and error as you go. But you'll find a system that works well for you. If it's a topic you know something about, you'll have an easier time of coming up with interesting questions. You can sometimes do better by having your subject provide the questions. This works really well when you're doing an executive's bio, or a podcast interview.

If you're interviewing someone who's an expert in a field you don't know much about, it's a good idea to be sure to get the expert's input on your interview questions. Otherwise, you could easily miss something important.

If you don't understand what they're talking about during your interview, make sure to get clarification. I read this great way to get a simpler explanation without looking like a total doofus. Just say, "Great. Now, tell me why this would matter to most people." Works every time.

For press releases, and I do a lot of those, it's a good idea to have a standardized list of questions you can send to the client. They complete it, and you write from their answers.

Here's the list of questions I always use:

- Tell me about your business.

- **What are your qualifications?**

- What are your specialties?

- What does your ideal client want?

- What do you do better than your competitors?

- What do you offer? Any special offers?

- Do you have any community involvement or professional affiliations?

- We'll need a quote relevant to your press release (something about your business, new addition, an honor or award, etc.)

- We'll also need to include a few lines about your company's history. Please include your tagline if you have one.

- Now the details: Name, address, phone, fax, email, and website for your business

- Contact person

How Does Ghostwriting Work?

Most of what I do is ghostwriting. There's not much glory – no by-lines, no feathers in the cap – but there is money in it! Projects include books, e-books, articles, and even speeches. A couple of times I've done autobiographies for people.

A few times I've written for very high-profile, highly successful people who know their stuff, but are too busy to write their own book about it. Or maybe they speak about it better than they'd write about it.

Content

There are a few challenges with ghostwriting. First, sometimes the content they want on paper exists only in their minds. It's hard to get it out, then into your mind, then into your document. You have to have a plan in place to achieve the brain dump you'll need to produce what they want. Very smart ghostwriting clients come to the table with a good outline, a draft (even if it's messy and incomplete), or a recording or transcript so you can work independently.

If they don't have this, you're looking at a LOT of interviews, and a LOT of rewrites – in other words, a project you don't really want. Think about it – how on earth would you write someone's life story if you don't know anything about them? Unless they're up for something fictionalized, you've got to have a lot of information to get it right.

Pricing

Another challenge is pricing. If you somehow manage to land a gig ghostwriting a celebrity's autobiography, you're probably going to need an agent to negotiate a fair price for you.

The book's probably getting published, and will probably rake in a mint! How will you feel if you did the whole thing for a couple thousand dollars? If your client is an "ordinary" person, you don't really have that challenge. But you do want to build a clause into your contract about revisions, time frame, etc. It might be worth having an attorney look at.

People decide to "write" their story for a lot of different reasons – but for most people, it's a once-in-a-lifetime task. They don't know what they're doing, and the process can be pretty frustrating. You could have this book lingering for months or years.

Again, not an effective way to build a business.

Confidentiality

The final challenge is confidentiality. You'll usually need to sign a non-disclosure agreement (NDA). Your client doesn't want you running around saying you wrote that book! It's a little less sticky when it's a series of articles, mostly because there's no temptation to brag!

But if a client requests confidentiality, you MUST provide it if you agree to it.

This means the project doesn't go into your portfolio. You can mention it as you bid – but only vaguely. For example, I don't give the name of the big-time realtor who hired me to ghostwrite her book. But I say something like, "I recently completed a book on real estate for a very successful South Florida real estate investor."

This saves her neck and mine. Also, if you are lucky enough to find a freelance writer with a bigger business than yours, who wants to outsource to you, it will be a ghostwriting gig.

You will get paid! But that's it. It's a work for hire. You can't use it in your portfolio. You can't contact the client. You can't re-use the text.

How Many Drafts Should I Write?

This may stir some controversy. I know James Michener writes (by hand, I think!) his huge novels about seven times each. I know we learned in school that the first draft stinks and should be shredded or burned.

But I write most projects ONCE.

I'm not writing a novel. I'm not after the Pulitzer. I'm writing web content. And I'm good at it. So I'm not going to waste time perfecting and agonizing. If my client requests revisions, that's fine, but it's usually because they failed to communicate clearly about how they wanted the article to go.

It's very easy for some writers to get bogged down in perfectionism. If this is you, you need to either get over it, or find something else to do. Because you will not make your deadlines, which is the cardinal sin of freelance writing, if you're obsessing over every word.

In fact, if you're doing jobs for another freelance writer, and you miss a deadline, you're probably done for. They'll have to clean up your mess, complete your work, and they'll never trust you to make a deadline again. Speed and competence are your friends. We're not churning out literary masterpieces here – although if you want to do that, you may be able to support your habit through your business, on your own time.

Here's an interesting experiment.

Do an article as quickly as you can – with complete focus, doing the very best you can within a tight timeframe. Even set a timer and see what you come up with. Send it to your client, using these specific words: "Here's a draft of your article. Please let me know if you need any changes."

You may be shocked how many times you'll get this response: "Great! Looks good. Invoice me."

Lesson learned? You could have spent double or triple that amount of time on that article – for nothing.

Now I'm not talking about sending sloppy work. Make sure your grammar's good, your spelling is correct, and that you've given it a good once-over before you send it off. But you'll get better and faster at all of that as you go.

How Do You Write an SEO Article?

Keyword, or search engine optimized articles are an art form unto themselves. Here's the basic explanation. Search engines, like Google, Yahoo, and Alta Vista (there are many more, but these are some biggies) send out something called spiders to crawl through the whole internet.

These spiders go into a web page and say, "Hmm, what's this about? What words appear a lot? Oh. Okay. This page is about (whatever). Let's make sure it comes up if someone searches for (whatever)."

So, since people who have websites want traffic, they want to make sure the search engines recognize the site as being relevant to that particular keyword. Different search engines use different criteria to determine whether a page is relevant.

Some want to see that keyword in the title, some want a certain keyword density (usually anywhere from 2% – 5%), and all want to be sure the page is high-quality and not full of junk.

Unscrupulous SEO companies produce volumes of pages that are absolute junk. They are articles that are basically a group of keywords strung together with no real content. What happens to these pages is that they're usually taken down, banned, or buried.

So your SEO clients want good quality articles that are also attractive to the search engines. The text should read well, even though you've used the keyword many times.

Density is this: If a client wants 3% keyword density, you take the total number of words in the article (usually about 500), and make sure that for every 100 words, you've used the keyword 3 times. So that article would feature that keyword 15 times in all.

Pretty simple, right?

Well….maybe not!

It can be a challenge to get it in there while making it sound human. It's even harder if the client needs an entire keyword phrase! I've got one who needed "articles about SEO techniques and web hosting" – those specific words in that order – to the tune of 5% density! Was it my best article ever? No. But I know I did it as well as it could possibly be done!

Tips on SEO Writing

Here are a few SEO writing tips:

- Stick to the word count. If you go over, you've got to fit that keyword in more frequently! For a 500 word article that runs into 600 words, at 5% density, you've got to fit the keyword in another 5 times. Ugh!

- Use the keyword in the title.

- Use the keyword in bullet points to introduce each section. For example, if the keyword is "how to improve your golf stroke" you could make bullet points like: "Tip #1 on How to Improve Your Golf Stroke" – as an easy way to get some of those keywords in.

How Do I Learn to Write Sales Copy?

This, my friends, is a cultivated skill. It takes practice. It takes research. It takes an understanding of how people think.

Essentially, your copy should answer the reader's burning question, which is, "What's in it for me?"

You have about three seconds to capture their attention with your headline. If you don't – click! You have another ten seconds to draw them in and make them want to read more. They skim, scan, and scroll their way through your text – and you never know what they will pause to read word-for-word. The testimonials? The checklist of benefits? The headlines? The guarantee? The call to action? They've all got to be good.

I recommend getting some sales letter templates and learning by example. (If you can, get your hands on one of Dr. Joe Vitale's Hypnotic Writing products.) Obviously, you can't copy and paste – your client will fire you immediately because you'll be sending the same sales letter they've actually received or stumbled across! The templates will guide you, give you examples to follow, and help you make sure you've got all of the elements.

Can You Write to Sell? Show Them!

After a while, I landed a slew of copywriting gigs doing sales letters. Always exciting, because they're kind of fun – in a sick, twisted, Sudoku-like way, anyway. Sales copy exercises a lot more neurons, in my opinion, than articles or ebooks. It's kind of like playing a game of Stratego or something.

One of my new clients said something that really jolted me.

You see, he'd gotten an avalanche of proposals for this project – a direct mail piece. But he said he could have tossed most of them for one simple reason – these writers violated the basic rules of copywriting, right when their proposals should have been shining examples of sales copy mastery.

I knew exactly what he was going to say.

These writers may have had experience writing sales copy – or maybe not. But even if they had no experience, he might never have known – if they followed one simple rule: answer your prospect's question, "What's in it for me?"

They applied for a gig in which their words would have to get people to take action. That requires showing those people how it's in their best interest to make a move. But what they didn't realize is that their proposal should have done the same thing – get the client to take action (hiring them).

The proposals this guy got were mostly filled with "we we" – you know, "we did this, we went here for school, we worked for this client." Instead, these writers would have done much better to just show him that they 'get' what he's after – results. They should have demonstrated that they know how to dig down to find the triggers that'll make prospects take action.

When you're trying to land a sales copy gig, demonstrate your powers of persuasion in your proposal. If you can do this effectively – and it does take practice – not only will your proposal rise to the top, but your fees will, too!

Formatting Your Sales Letter – Icing on the Cake

There you are at a little kid's birthday party. The presents have been opened. The song sung. The candles extinguished. You try to look coolly patient while you wait for someone to pass you a slice of cake, your mouth watering and your vision laser focused on each plate as it is passed from hand to hand. Finally, your slice arrives. Fork plunges into this guilty indulgence, mouth awaits the sugary bliss of confection – until you realize you got one of those pieces that's almost all icing and no cake.

Hey, I'm all about icing – in harmonious balance with cake, anyway. But too much, and your teeth are left on edge, your palate wishing for something more substantive.

It's the same way with sales letter formatting.

Last time we looked at a super easy, systematic way to produce a compelling sales letter by using Joe Vitale's Hypnotic Writing Swipe File. I clocked myself a few days ago, just to see how long it takes using this method: start to finish (and this time with kind of a strange software product that I had a hard time getting an angle on) to produce a seven-page letter, it was 3.5 hours. Not bad, and I'm still perfecting the technique.

That was for content. The formatting? About 10 minutes. For many sales letter writers, it's almost the opposite – and the result is as unsatisfying as a slice of cake that's all icing.

You've read letters like this. Full of typos. All about "me and we" rather than how the product will actually help you, the reader. Some even contain traces of completely unrelated letters that were "borrowed" to use as a template – the writer didn't even bother to read all the way through to make sure it all made sense! But at first glance, the formatting made it look like an okay letter.

So, the first rule of sales letter formatting is to have good content. After that, you can worry about fonts, white spaces, highlighting, and font colors. Here's a list of ten tips you can use to format with the best of them:

1. Remember that people skim, scan, and scroll. Use your formatting to make it so a reader gets the whole story even by just reading the parts that are bold or highlighted.

2. Sans serif fonts work best online. Serif fonts work best for direct mail. Verdana and Times Roman are good examples of each of these.

3. Your main headline should be about 18 points – and could be black or red.

4. Subheads should be 14 or 16; try both to see which looks best.

5. Main text should be 12.

6. Use underlining and italics very sparingly – they're hard to read.

7. Add extra white space to surround subheads.

8. You can bold some of the words in your text blocks, just make sure it makes sense to emphasize them. Same thing for adding yellow highlights.

9. In a bullet list (features and benefits), try bolding alternate bullet points if there are more than about five in the list.

10. Format LAST. Read through your letter without any formatting and make sure it's good that way.

Remember the difference between cake and icing, and bake the cake first. Your sales letters will be a lot more solid, and the results will be sweet!

How Do I Handle a Really Big Project?

You will get these from time to time. It's nice to have a good balance between quick little articles and bigger ongoing projects. But it's easy to get bogged down and really overwhelmed when you're working on a big one.

Everyone says you should just cut it into bite-sized pieces and go from there. And it's generally good advice, except that now you're left juggling a lot of small pieces – and it's very easy to forget where you were when you left off, and what you still need to do.

A work in progress is usually not all that pretty. But the good thing is that you're probably the only one who's going to see it. So do whatever you have to do to keep the project organized and moving forward.

So, You Want to Write a Book?

Freelance writers, it's bound to happen to you sooner or later. You'll get a client who wants you to write a book; or you'll just decide to do one for yourself. It's (happily) inevitable – and a little scary, at least the first time around.

Let's do the little happy dance of joy first, though! My goodness, THIS is what writing is all about, right? (OK, let's pretend for a moment that your book is actually about something you're passionately interested in – not about removing cat urine odors from your home (big smile to Michelle).) I mean, book writing is the big time, the crème de la crème, the raison d'etre for writers. (Wow, I must be excited if I'm dusting off my old French vocabulary.)

Now that we've gotten that out of our systems, you know what comes next – complete panic. The "Oh my goodness, I got the job. Now what??" kind of panic that only comes from doing something we've always wanted to do – but for money. Breathe. Breathe again.

With both extremes fully expressed, it's time to get down to work.

Where do you start?

Remember those horrible English class projects where you had to carry around a stack of index cards, writing just one thought on each? (For the younger freelance writers out there, yes, this was before computers – and cell phones, dvds, and even cable TV.) The great news is that that awful index card system is dead forever. The underlying principle, however, is alive and kicking.

You're going to start by making a list. In no particular order, brainstorm 25 different topics you need to cover in your book. (Note: if you're doing a book for a client, have them do this part – this way you're certain you've covered everything they think is most important.) Under each of these 25 topics, you're going to list four subtopics.

Now you've got a pretty nice little outline going. Time to put the points in a logical order.

Doing the actual writing

Pick a point – any point – and start writing. If you're aiming for a 200 page book, you'll write about two pages for each subtopic. That means for a 100 page book, you write one page for each subtopic.

Because we're blessed with all the benefits of word processing programs, you can write and save, write and save, write and save until you've got all your topics covered – before you ever have to do any formatting.

Getting it all in order

The next task is to break the topics into chapters. They're already organized into some reasonably logical order, so all you have to do is group them into related topics. Make sure they flow together nicely. You may need to add introductory or concluding remarks to each chapter.

The finishing touches

You're going to need to add some other bookish elements to your now hefty work of verbal art. An introduction, a conclusion, a Table of Contents (easily done with some practice using Word's headings functions), an index if necessary, and any other little extras such as acknowledgments, disclaimers, dedications, etc. come next. You'll also need to add formatting including page numbers, bolding, headers and/or footers, and of course a title page.

Practically painless, right?

It's a method that helps keep you on track, organized, and also enables you to write on whatever section you feel inspired to tackle on any particular day. Don't know whether it would work for fiction, but it might!

Project Management for E-Book Writing

Here's what I do for big e-books, and it's all within one document.

Again, I start with the outline – points and sub-points. They're not necessarily in the order they'll end up in at the end.

I pick something to start on, and create a new page after the outline. At the top of the page, I include the number and letter that correspond to the outline. So, 6 – b – Your assistant, for example.

Write and save, write and save. Go back to the outline and highlight point 6b in yellow. Don't feel like writing any more from point 6, so I'm moving onto point 18. Make a new page: 18 – d – Chamber of Commerce. Write and save, write and save. Highlight point 18d on the outline in yellow.

Hmm. It's time to go to bed.

Oh, but I just got a great idea about a quote or something. Do you write it on a scrap of paper? Nope. Go to page one of the document, above the outline, and write: Get a quote about a tightrope walker (or whatever!).

Next day comes, and I'm back to work. Groggy without my coffee (just gave it up – HELP MEEE!!!), I vaguely remember something about a circus or something... Oh yes, here it is – right on page one: get a quote about a tightrope walker. OK. Where was I? What have I done already? Well, I can see by the highlights that I've done points 6b and 18d. Moving right along!

Then, when you've got a lot of the project done, it's time to get it into chapters. You go back to the outline and start thinking about groupings of related points. All the ones about sales get the heading highlighted green. All the ones about administrative stuff get the heading highlighted red. You do some cutting and pasting, and now it's starting to take shape.

Save and Back Up Your Work

Oh yes, a word about saving and backing up.

I hope you'll never see the screen of death that says your computer just crashed, because it's stress nobody needs. Obviously you should save your work often. But as a backup, use an offsite backup!

Mozy.com offers a free backup system that I recommend. You can customize it to backup the files you want, as often as you want. Very cool. The idea is that if something were to happen, you can go into the site and download all your goodies again. Sure beats having a coronary!

11 Words That Will Make Your Business Easier

Ever had a 'bad' client?

For those of you just starting out, I hear you: "BAD client? I'd be happy to have ANY client!"

Well, hang in there with us, because you'll have your share, too! And if you're prepared in advance, maybe you can flatten the learning curve a bit.

I had one project that I'd love you to learn from. I'd been working on it for a month.

OK, so what?

Well, it should have taken one week tops. And it got to the point I felt like I might just puke if I had to look at it again – or if I got another call from this client asking for yet another round of revisions.

Confession: Basically, I want her to pay up, go away, and go away happy – but mostly just go away.

It'll happen to you, too.

This whole topic opens up a whole can of worms:

- How can I make this a win-win for us both?

- What gut feelings did I ignore as I got myself into this project?

- What about when I know I'm right and my client is wrong?

- What effect will I allow it to have on my business (and my sanity!)?

- How can I choose better next time?

- What tweaks can I make to my systems to make sure this doesn't happen again?

I'm still wrestling with some of these, but can possibly spare you some agony in the future by sharing some insights on the others.

Here's what I suggest:

- First of all, be grateful. After all, I HAVE a bad client. That means I've got a client base. It also means most of my clients are good – or else this one wouldn't stand out.

- Second, take responsibility. I chose this client as much as they chose me. We talked at length before starting, and I'm the one who made the decision to move forward. This means I can also choose better next time!

- Third, stand by your commitment. I signed a contract, and will honor it to the end. While doing this means I might sacrifice some sleep, the fun of working on a 'good' project, and even my appetite, at least I don't have to sacrifice my integrity!

- Fourth, check out your contract verbiage. I knew there was a phrase I should include – but never got around to it, because it had never been an issue before. It reads something like this: "The writing fee includes X rounds of revisions within 30 days." With these 11 words, the whole problem could have been avoided!

- Fifth, about being 'right': Yes, I wrote some absolutely killer copy – the first go-round. Yes, to be honest, after all the revisions and client input, I think it's now less than stellar. Yes, I'm the copywriter and she's not. But, she's the client, and my goal is to serve rather than to be right.

Hey, 'bad' clients happen.

It should be no surprise. The only question that remains is, how will you deal with it? Will you allow it to derail your business, life, and mood? Or will you redeem the situation, create value in it, and learn to make better choices next time?

Working Writer Snooty Writer?

"Sorry for the wait. Ms. LaPointe will speak with you now," says my fantasy assistant to yet another potential client begging me to write some copy for him.

There's a line of clients out the virtual door, and they're breaking out the sleeping bags and pup tents to wait to talk to me about their projects. When they finally arrive at the front of the line, it's with gifts in hand.

Ahhhhh, to be so popular.

Think you've got to reach superstar status to be choosy about your clients? No way.

Sure, when you're just starting, you'll probably kiss some frogs just to build a portfolio. Eventually, though, you'll get to pick and choose your clients. They'll have to pass muster to make it onto your calendar.

Except that sometimes, The Client from the Pit sneaks in and leaves you wondering whether your "PITA" detector needs a tune-up.

You're left with a client who seems impossible to please, whose feedback leaves bruises, and who you'd probably pay just to make him go away. If only you could recognize this client BEFORE you take the project!

It's really not about being snooty – it's more about abundance and self-respect. There are an infinite number of writing gigs out there; why on earth would you choose the ones that sap the lifeblood out of you?

Top 5 Signs You Should Run – and Fast

1. **The Late Night Caller.**
    Unless this client is calling from Australia AND does not own a watch, there is no reason on earth you should get a call way after hours. Think it doesn't happen? I got one last night from an ex-prospective client.

2. **The Long Talker.**
    This client seems to think you need her entire life history in order to write a press release. She doesn't come up for air. You begin to realize that IF you take this gig, you'd darned well better charge by the hour.

3. **The Minutiae Man.**
    You can see this one coming a mile away. Even the project description is so exacting, so detailed, that you have to focus on it like you're about to do surgery. What are the odds he's going to be easy to please?

4. **The Walking Wounded.**
    This client's project description begins with a tale of woe, how

she and her partner have invested all their time and money into this project. How it's six months behind schedule, and they've been done wrong by everyone involved. Unless you have a Rescuer complex, you should pass. This project is a train wreck, and you'll find yourself picking up after everyone else.

5. **The Big Talker.**
This is the one who says his budget is really small for **this** part of the project, but promises that if you do well for a tiny fee, he's got lots more work for you. Do you honestly want "lots more" of that?

This is one I forgot about for a while. I had a client who promised to keep me and my firm so busy we'd never have to look for work again.

Tempting?

You bet! Now the catch was this – the rate of pay was about half what we usually do. And the deadlines were about half what we usually do.

Hmm… this was sounding less appealing.

But I bit anyway, contrary to that little voice that said: "RUN!" And it didn't take long to realize this was a big mistake. From now on, the rule is this: you can get your writing cheap, fast, or good… but not all three.

6. **The "Disobedient" Client.**
OK, the title for that one's tongue-in-cheek, but you'll understand. We all have different ways that we best absorb information. For some, if they hear something, it's burned into their brains forever. Others (like me) need to see information. Tell me something, and I'm going to try to remember – but you take your chances. I always ask clients to email me with details. If I've got to take notes as you speak, I'm missing something. If I don't take notes, I can't depend on my memory serving it up a week from now – intact.

Yes, of course, I aim to please – but short of having our phone call transcribed, I'm not sure how to accommodate the client who won't just email.

So what's to become of these clients?

Believe me, there are plenty of writers out there who would be thrilled to land a gig from them. They'll be fine.

You, however, who are building a thriving writing business, you can do better. And you've got my permission to be a Working Writer Snooty Writer.

Build Your Portfolio and Pad Your Wallet at the Same Time

For beginning freelance writers, the whole concept of getting a portfolio is a lot like the old chicken and the egg question. You need a portfolio to get a paying gig – but you need a paying gig to build a portfolio. Right?

Wrong!

At least on that second part. You do need a portfolio, of course – but the pieces you put in it don't necessarily need to be paid works.

I usually recommend that new writers start out by adding articles to their portfolios. Articles are some of the most common writing projects out there, and if you can provide good sample articles to potential clients, they can get a good look at your style and voice.

What should you write about?

Honestly, it doesn't really matter. The goal is not so much to show how much you know about any particular subject. Freelancers are famous for being able to do quick research to be able to write intelligently about nearly any topic.

What's more important than the topic is having an understanding of what your prospective clients are looking for, why they need articles in the first place.

My guess is that 9 out of 10 clients who order articles are using them for article marketing – a very effective, relatively inexpensive way to draw traffic to their websites. Basically it works like this: they submit articles to an article directory, webmasters re-publish these articles, people search for info on that specific topic and find the article, read it, follow the link to the website, and eventually buy something.

From that quick description, what do you think clients are looking for?

- Articles that are well-written. If the article is a literary disaster area, nobody is going to want to read it, much less follow it to find out more!

- Articles that are interesting. If readers, known for 3-second attention spans, click away after the first paragraph, they'll never end up on the client's website, much less buying anything.

- Articles that are conversational. Unless you're specializing in technical writing, the articles your clients want most read like people actually speak (okay, depending on the person in question – no profanity or obscure slang, please).

Now, for the "pad your wallet at the same time" part

If you're going to create articles for your portfolio, why not do it in a way that can earn you some money while you're at it? There's an entire realm of internet marketing called affiliate marketing. You can try your hand at it and build your portfolio at the same time. Basically, you pick a product or website that has an affiliate program in place, and join the program. Then you write articles to promote the product. Publish them (and include them in your portfolio!), and before long, you'll have people clicking and buying because they read your article.

You can go to www.affsphere.com for a great report on this. Anik Singal's not a freelance writer, so he didn't think about the potential goldmine we writers are sitting on (after all, we don't have the expense of hiring a writer!) or about multipurposing these articles by using them in a portfolio while they're also out there on the internet earning money. But his report (at this writing, about $5-10) also answers questions like:

- How do I find a good product to promote with my articles?

- How do I know whether it'll actually make money?

- What do readers want to read?

- How do I write a great title, article, and resource box?

- Where should I submit these articles?

The cardinal rule of writing for yourself (don't try this with work for clients) is: write it once, use it in as many different ways as you can. Sounds like a plan!

5 Easy Ways to Build Your Portfolio:

1. The friends and family plan. If anyone you know has a business, ask whether they'd like some writing done - even for free, if necessary. Do a press release, a brochure, some website content - anything you need for your portfolio.

2. Work for f.ree - just for now. Your church, PTO, Brownie Troop, or any other nonprofit ALWAYS needs help getting the word out about events, fundraisers, etc.

3. Take a class and show off your homework - after it's graded and cleaned up, anyway. This is how graphic artists, interior designers, and many other pros create their first portfolio, too.

4. Stand in the place that you work. If writing is a moonlighting gig for you right now, see what you can do to help your current (soon to be ex-!) employer in the area of writing.

5. Write real copy for a made-up business. For example, if you're at the dentist office all the time, you probably know all you'd need to know to 'sell' your dentist. Write about this dentist, but give different particulars.

Chapter 7 – In and On Your Business

There are some things in life we can do alone just fine.

There are other things we need a team of people for if we're going to do it right.

Running a profitable business is one of those things. No matter how solitary writing can be, and I know lots of writers who love the Lone Ranger life, this is something where you need a team if you're going to really reach your potential.

Is there really any such thing as a self-made success?

I say "no way!"

You can try building your writing business this way, but it's a sure recipe for burn-out, costly mistakes, and a lot of unnecessary headaches. For certain, it's not putting good time mastery principles to use.

You see, one huge part of using your time wisely is knowing when not to use YOUR time. To get most things done, you need either time or money. As we've discussed before, time is really your most precious commodity. It can't be replaced.

In your writing business, there are four levels of competency:

- Incompetent: These are things you absolutely can't do. Even if you worked really hard to improve, you'd only make marginal progress. Things like this might include setting up your tax and legal entity structure, doing your books, printing your marketing materials – all kinds of things people routinely hire a specialist to do for them.

- Competent: These are the things you're okay at, but not great. They might include running errands to the bank, the post office, the copy store. You could do them, but so could anyone else.

- Excellence: These are things you do exceptionally well. Maybe it's writing SEO articles, e-books, website content, or brochure text. You're skilled at these types of tasks, and do them better than most people you know.

- Genius: This is something you do better than anyone else – it's where your gift lies. It's really something special. Ideally, you'll figure out what this is, and be able to spend the bulk of your time doing it. It can take years – decades even – to figure it out though.

Now, if you're building a writing business, where do you think you should spend most of your time? Filing? Filling out deposit slips? Balancing a checkbook? Or, how about actually WRITING?

But, all those other things need to be done, too! And some of them are really, really important to the success of your business.

For example, if you're working as a sole proprietor, you're going to take a punch in the gut when tax time rolls around. Unless you're an accountant or attorney, you probably don't know a whole lot about tax entities (and you probably don't care to!). But having the right entity in place makes a huge difference in how much of your writing income you actually get to keep. So, are you going to go enroll in a college class to learn about tax law? Leave that kind of stuff to the specialists. It's not worth your time. Good time management means you'll pay someone else to take care of this stuff for you, so you are free to do what you do best.

So who do you need on your team?

You can divide the people on your team into people who work *in* your business and people who work *on* your business.

People Working In Your Business

- **Other writers, graphic designers, and web designers.**
  There will come a point when you will be too busy. When you're just starting out, that doesn't even seem possible – but it will definitely happen. You can only write so much per day, and you'll find yourself turning down work. Unless you build a team.
  This is a slow process if you do it correctly. It's a big deal to have another writer working with you. You've got to be in synch; you've got to have the same writing style; you've got to be able to trust that writer to meet the deadline and to do the job you would have done yourself. There are a lot of writers out there who want to write, but who don't want to market. They're great at getting the job done, but don't want to go get the job. When the time comes, you want to find them.

  Now be clear on this, you are still absolutely responsible for the end product that your client gets. You may have to clean up messes now and then. But if you can find and/or train other writers to do what you do, you can really watch your business take off.

  I'll save the nuts and bolts for this topic for another book. Just know that eventually, you'll want to head in this direction.

- **A virtual assistant, or VA.**
  There are parts of your writing business that don't require your personal attention. These are necessary tasks, but you shouldn't necessarily be doing them yourself. At some point as your business grows, you'll want to outsource some of the administrative stuff. This is the perfect opportunity to use a VA.

  Your VA can handle any clearly defined task you've got: billing, bidding, proofreading, submitting work, and submitting press releases and articles to directories to name a few. You can look on Craigslist.org or on a freelance job board, or even ask around as you network to find an assistant.

Hire them as an independent contractor – they usually have multiple clients, so this is how they tend to work. And delegate everything that you can to them. Your assistant's first job will actually be to create a procedure manual based on your documentation. We'll get into that in a bit.

- **An editor.**
  It's really good to have a fresh pair of eyes go over your work one last time before you send it to a client. Nothing's more embarrassing than having a big typo in the middle of a headline! Find an editor who can work quickly, on short notice, and provide a thorough edit in just a little bit of time. Make sure to provide a style sheet so they can check the work against the specs.

People Working On Your Business

- **A good CPA.**
  It's one of those things where you figure they're all pretty much the same. Having sat for the CPA exam once (didn't pass), and knowing how hard it is, I have the utmost respect for anyone who's passed it.

  These people can hold more information in their brains than I could hold in a bucket! But, they are not all equal. Some are more knowledgeable about different areas of accounting than others. You want a really good CPA who does work for a lot of entrepreneurs. You want them because they can give excellent advice, they know about the entities you're looking into, and they're a bit more aggressive than many other CPA's.

  Some will ask for a retainer in addition to the tax preparation fees. Others will ask to do your bookkeeping all along throughout the year. Just don't go with the first one you call, and hope for the best. Interview them. Make sure they've worked with clients in a somewhat similar situation.

- **A bookkeeper.**
  Back to the darned math! You know, I love writing, marketing, editing, and dealing with clients. What I hate is recording numbers. I don't want to look at QuickBooks. I barely want to take the time to print out my invoices and payment information. I'd be completely fine leaving my bank statements in their original envelopes.

  This is why I had to hire a bookkeeper. I chuck stuff into a file folder and give it to him once a month. He comes back with a beautiful set of reports. I give him a check, and we start all over for the next month. Having all of my info in such tidy shape saves me a bundle with my CPA, too. If I had to pay his office to do this maintenance work, it would be a lot more expensive.

  If I sent him my info without having it processed by the bookkeeper, my CPA would probably fire me! Again, I could probably do this on my own, but would rather remove my own appendix. Look at the highest best use of your time.

- **A coach.**
  Reading a book is nice.
  Going to a seminar is nice.
  Listening to a teleseminar is also nice.

  But those are light years away from working one-on-one with a coach. Coaching isn't counseling – they're not there to make you feel better and hold your hand (although sometimes that happens!). The point of counseling is to ask what the next step is to move you toward your goals, and to help you take that step – then to hold you accountable for doing it on your own.

  Look for a coach who's worked with freelance writers before, if possible, because they'll know a lot more about how you do what you do.

Other People on Your Team

- **Household help.**
  This may seem like an indulgence, and it might not be workable for you for a while, but keep it in mind as a goal. Once you're busy with writing projects, you can appreciate the value of your hourly rate.

  How long does it take you to clean your house? Even if it's just two hours a week (then you must have one neat family!), at a rate of $75 per hour, you're losing $150 each time you clean. If you hire a cleaning crew for $75, and they knock out the whole house in an hour, you've done a few good things.

  You freed yourself up to spend that hour earning money. You've saved money in the long run. And you employed other people, helping them to provide for their own needs. All this, without even getting into how nice it is to have your house in order and clean without having to do it yourself.

  Always ask yourself whether what you're doing is the highest best use of your time. If the answer is no, hire someone else to do it.

About Your Assistant

As you start your business, you'll find that you wear every hat in it. You're the marketer, the administrator, the billing department, the quality control department, salesperson, oh yes – and the writer! We've talked a little about making sure you're using your time in the best way possible.

Part of that strategy involves hiring an assistant. You'll know when the time is right. You won't want to do it until you have some steady money coming in. But once that's reliable, it's time to start looking. Your assistant doesn't need to be full-time, by any means. You can easily get by with having someone help out just a few hours a week.

Here's where it gets tricky. Once you get really good at doing all the things you have to do in your business, it will feel like it's just easier to keep doing them than to train someone else to do it.

After all, what if you have to go back and fix it if they do it wrong? It's kind of like teaching your children to fold bath towels. Probably it's not going to come out the way you'd do it, but it's really not bad at all – and it's better to have the help than not. Fortunately, most assistants are adults, and easily trainable!

So how do you train someone? This is an ingenious method my coach passed along to me. Once you've got any one method down pat, say, your bidding, write a procedure manual about how to do bidding. Make it thorough enough that someone who's never done it can do it right by following only your written instructions. Write it with a pen and paper (I know, what's that?!). Your assistant's first job is to type it up.

This is a great way for your assistant to get a first glimpse of how to do that task. Then have your assistant do some bidding for you. Check it before it's submitted – just this once. Then make bidding part of the assistant's job.

You keep going with other tasks someone else can do, like:

- Proofreading

- Invoicing

- Bank deposits

- Filing

- Paying bills

- Follow-up with local contacts

In the end, you have these jobs done – the way you would have done them; you have an assistant who's well-trained; you have a procedural manual you can use to train another assistant (if yours moves on). Or, if you are so pleased with your assistant that you decide to promote him or her up to another position (marketing, maybe?), your assistant can train the next assistant you hire.

Do I Need a Website?

Yes, and no.

Beware – this is one puddle of quick sand that's easy to fall into – and never get out. That's why this question is buried all the way in Chapter 6! Do NOT bother with a website until you have projects under your belt. You will probably obsess, pay a lot of money, get frustrated, and throw in the towel before you ever even get going if you mess with a website first.

Now, once you've got an actual business going, it's a different story. A website is still not absolutely necessary – you could easily do without. But it's a nice thing to have, and may help you with marketing.

I have one (okay, I have a few – it's kind of addicting – another reason to wait until you've got a business going), but it really serves more as a place where people can check out some samples. It's like an online portfolio.

I have actually gotten some clients by having it, and it's always a surprise when it happens. Why? Because the site's not fully developed – you see, I'm too busy writing to put time into doing the search engine marketing I'd need to do to compete with the (at this writing) 2,750,000 other sites that come up if you Google "freelance writer". It's just not the way I get most of my clients, so it's not worth the time it would take to try to get onto page one!

Building a Website

With that in mind, I recommend getting a very simple site building program like <u>XSite Pro</u> so you can do it yourself without it looking like you did it yourself. As someone who's not especially techy, I was surprised to find that even I could build a website (or a dozen!) pretty easily.

You can get a domain name and hosting from <u>GoDaddy.com</u> for just a few dollars a month. Plus, they're very, very helpful there – they've never once laughed at me when I've asked what must be really dumb questions. I like that in a company!

So what do you put on your site? Use a lot of the text you have on your brochure. Include PDF's of your portfolio. Have your contact info, including an email address at that site (for example, info@workingwriterhappywriter.com). Do NOT put your personal email address – you will get more junk email than you've ever dreamed possible.

Pretty simple. You can improve it as you go, but it's probably not going to be your primary form of marketing, so don't spend a lot of time on it.

Can You Grab that Call?

Working at home is wonderful in so many ways. But there's one challenge you'll encounter very soon – your phone.

Your phone's a blessing and a curse all at once.

Sure, you can use it to get work. Dialing for dollars, I think they call it. Not that you have to cold call anyone, ever, to get writing gigs – but some people actually enjoy it. And our friend Peter Bowerman (*Well–Fed Writer* series) swears by cold calling as an integral way to jump start your business.

It's also good for quick consults with your clients and prospects. Lots of them want to kind of get a feel for you as a person and a writer before they hire you. Or, they want to chat a bit about the nuances of their project. And all of that's good, too.

But your phone can be a real bear sometimes, too.

For example, if you put your home number on your business card or your website, you take the risk that a potential client will call you, and your eight-year-old will answer the phone. Of course, she'll say something like, "Mommy can't come to the phone right now. She's cleaning up cat puke. Can she call you back?" – or worse!

Or, your card could fall into the hands of telemarketers. And that's bad enough if you've listed a land line. But what if you've printed your cell phone number on the card? You'll go through minutes like crazy – all for nothing.

The ideal situation would be to have your own staff answering and even screening your calls. Shoot, your clients would probably think you were really big stuff – a veritable Bob Bly! Imagine what that would do for your image?

Back to reality, though. Most of us don't have the budget for office staff – and frankly, if I had a bunch of staff, I'd really prefer to have an actual office at that point. And that would mean no more writing in my bunny slippers!

In the first edition of this book, I recommended getting a 'fake' phone number through a free service. Unfortunately, apparently that particular price point didn't exactly generate the revenues the site owner hoped! So they discontinued the service. So I went on a hunt for a replacement (and prepared to re-print my business cards).

I found a pretty darned good deal with this site called Ring Central, so I wanted to pass it along to you. You can sign up for a no-obligation, no-cost trial, too, which is cool. The monthly fee is under $10 – not bad at all. The service also offers fax capabilities, which is a huge plus if you don't want to crowd your work area with a bunch of equipment. You can also get a toll-free number and/or a local number, which makes it even easier for your clients to reach you.

Use your new number to give your writing business a nice touch. Your clients will be impressed with your professionalism. Your kids will live a lot longer, too, since they won't be able to intercept your important calls!

What "Stuff" Do I Need?

Not much, actually. There are some standard things you probably already have. Make sure you have a fairly recent version of Word. If you're on dial-up Internet, get off and get high-speed. Get your fake phone number. A fax machine is very nice for the rare time you need it, but if you have a scanner, you can use that instead usually.

One gadget that's been helpful several times is a little digital voice recorder. There have been projects where I needed to record an interview in person, or a conference call that I wasn't leading (with their permission!). You can get one for about $25 at an office supply place, but I'd wait until it looks like you'll need it.

You will need some way to convert documents into PDF's. There's a great, free little conversion program called <u>Cute PDF</u> that's really, really easy to use. To make a PDF, you just go like you're going to print, but instead of sending the document to your printer, you send it to Cute PDF, and save the PDF.

Easy as pie.

Get – and WEAR – a Name Badge

A nametag is a glorious thing!

Aside from helping save you from the embarrassment of forgetting someone's name, they're also a great way to promote your business. You can get a good looking badge for about $10 online. It should feature your name, logo, and company name.

Go with the magnetic badge so you don't destroy your clothing. Keep it with you all the time, and wear it whenever possible. I wear mine to every networking event, my referral swap group, luncheons, to client meetings, and even when I go out to Staples. You just never know who you might meet – and it provides a great conversation starter.

Home Sweet Home? Or, Home Sweet Suite?

95% of all freelance writers work from home.

OK. I made that up, actually. But it sounds about right, doesn't it? After all, look at some of the advantages you enjoy if you work from home:

- No overhead expenses from rent

- No commute

- You can work in your jammies

- No eating-out lunch expenses

- Home office deduction on your taxes

- Perfect for parents – every day is bring your child to work day

Oh, wait – is that last one a benefit? Or is it a good reason to start checking out your local commercial real estate market? While it might seem like a no-brainer that a home office is the way to go, there are many writers who've made the move into "real" office space. In fact, at some point, you might find yourself weighing the location decision yourself.

It may be time to rent a space if:

- You need an administrative or marketing assistant. At some point, your business will grow so busy that you'll need to make choices about how you spend your time. Always, the question to ask is whether doing XYZ is truly the highest, best use of your time. When it's time to bring in regular help, you might want to move the office out of the bedroom. A commercial space will give you both the elbow room you'll need.

- You're working a LOT with local clients. An office won't necessarily attract foot traffic, but your operation will look 100% more professional if you're able to meet with clients somewhere that's not at your dining room table.

- You're having a hard time balancing a life and a business. You'll be far less tempted to find your keys, drive across town, and turn all the lights back on in your office after hours than you might be to pick your laptop up for one more peek before hitting the sheets. If you're finding it hard to avoid distraction, a move may help.

If you do decide to look at renting an office space, here are a few pointers I've picked up from writers who've made the move:

- Watch your budget. Don't over-spend on a space that's bigger than you need. Even if your company outgrows the space you rent now, it's better to upgrade then than to over-spend now.

- Look for a space within a smaller office park. In places like this, landlords may be more flexible about the price because they can't afford vacancies.

- Be sure to check with your insurer to see if you need additional coverage. Now that you've got clients coming to see you at your office, you may need more insurance.

Whether you work from home or make the move into the outside world, do it with a big smile. After all, how many businesses offer so many options? How many other businesses allow you to work when and where you want? The freelance writing life is sweet – wherever you live it.

Chapter 8 – What Else Can I Do to Earn Money with Words?

Oh, the many ways we have with words!

We've really been focused on commercial writing, because it's so plentiful and easy to get and to do (with some practice). But it's not the final word on making money from freelance writing. Here are a few other things you might consider:

But first, a little discussion on why you'd want to learn about some other ways to make money from writing.

"All It'll Cost Me Is Some Time"

Boy was that a familiar phrase back when I was wandering through the desert of home-based employment options. I remember it most vividly when I was in my custom-knitting phase. A complete yarn addict, I figured there was no way my kids could possibly wear every sweater, scarf, and pom-pom hat that flew off of my needles. Ever seeking a way to boost my stash of increasingly expensive fibers, and never yet dreaming someone could actually earn a living from writing, I decided to tap my fingers to be my business partners.

Sounded kind of glamorous, being a clothing designer. Sure sounded more profitable than my failed cigar box purse design business. And hey, I already had the yarn, so all it would cost me was some time.

The trouble all started when a friend asked me how many hours went into a sweater. (Darned Accountant! Had to ruin all the fun!)

"Ummm, well, actually about 16-20 hours." I knew the next questions she'd ask.

"How much is that alpaca yarn worth? How much do those cute little buttons cost? The little tags in the back with your brand on them? How much are you charging? Wow, so you're really working for minus $7 an hour!"

Why did she have to do that?

I knew the answers. And I knew they were going to reveal a big gaping hole in my business plan (which was non-existent, of course).

Every piece I sold put me further into the red.

But that wasn't even the worst of it.

You see, it all started with my skewed perception of the value of my time. I counted it as of less value than a bunch of wool and some cute little buttons. In evaluating my "business" assets, I put my time at the bottom of the list. A simple look at a calendar might have taught me something better:

Your time is your MOST valuable asset.

Why? Because it can't be replaced. Once it's gone, it's gone.

How's this little foray into fibers apply to freelance writers? Well, at least two ways:

1. Be mindful of your time, and guard it. If, instead of doing the things you know you need to do to move your business forward, you're futzing around, stop it. Work with focus. In my case, that means no phone, no email while I'm writing. If you write for free (or for peanuts), you'd better have a good reason in mind for doing so. There are times when it's a good idea – but if you're doing it because you don't value your time, please take another look.

2. I can't stress this enough: find a way to use your writing to earn residual, or passive income. If you get into info marketing, you're already leaps ahead of some marketers – at least in one important way. You can write! Which means you can write your own products, your own sales letters, your own articles.

Yes, there's a learning curve. And it's definitely not an overnight success thing. Ahhhh – so another thing that takes time. But the information is out there.

So, invest in yourself along the way and pick up some other skills, some other ways to use words to earn money.

Writing Specialist or Generalist?

Several writers have asked me some version of this question recently: "I landed a new gig. How much should I charge for (this project that I've never done before)?"

The answer comes in two parts.

The first part, I call "Ready, Fire, Aim" – you need to do your best to come up with a price that works for you and your client. Understand, though, that part of building a business is learning by experience (er, mistakes!). If you take a bath one a project, don't throw in the towel and fill out an application at McDonalds. It happens – even with lots of experience. Especially when you do something new. And it's okay. The value of the experience depends on what you do with what you learn. Keep notes on how long the project takes, what areas were challenging, what your hourly rate came out to, and how you'll charge the next time a similar project comes up.

During those projects where you take a bath, try to see it as receiving a paid (even if poorly paid) education. Get the most from every learning experience you get. Don't waste time feeling bitter or depressed because you made a pricing mistake. Do your very best on the project, and be grateful that you won't have to learn that same lesson again, because you'll "aim" better next time.

The second part of the answer speaks to having a writing specialty. When you're first starting out, you'll probably take just about any project that comes your way. Good plan – you get to build your portfolio, iron out your pricing, and learn which projects you enjoy and do best.

It won't take long before you'll develop a real knack for one type of writing over another. I know that on my writing team, most of my writers have specialties. Some specialties revolve around content. One went to law school, others are moms, one is a yoga instructor, and another was a teacher. Several of them also have project specialties. One writer has become my go-to for press releases. She's fast, does an excellent job, and knows the different styles like the back of her hand – I don't have to explain the project; she just gets it. She writes them just like I would, so it's a no-brainer for me to tap her when I need help. Another writer is getting really good with sales letters. Another does e-books and articles. Another is an awesome proofreader.

Do these writers do other types of projects? Of course! But they've become sought after by clients (me, in this case!) because they've got a specialty down cold.

The goal is to focus, but not to have tunnel vision. Learn new skills when you've got the opportunity. But also pursue excellence in a couple of areas of specialization.

Editing

It's writing's first-cousin.

For the most part, the easiest gigs to get for editing are for aspiring writers. Kind of ironic, but in a good way. Many of these people are truly talented, and have as good a shot at getting published as anyone else with some talent. Some are truly horrible writers. Most are in-between.

You can find a lot of these projects on the job boards. One board I used to use a lot is Editfast.com. I got a few projects, and had some fun, but I like the way Guru is set up better.

The thing with editing projects on the boards is that most of them never move forward. It's best to check the client's profile – have they done anything before on the site? Have they actually gone the distance and paid someone to edit something? Many of them have. Many have not.

You'll find a lot of "I've written my autobiography/a children's book/a novel and need it cleaned up "a little."" Proceed with caution! And charge more than you think you should.

Another place you're likely to get editing gigs is academia. Especially with students whose first language is not English. Doctoral students in particular are often looking for help polishing their theses before handing them in.

This is a high-pressure gig because there are very strict stylistic guidelines you've got to comply with, tight deadlines (procrastinating students!), and the awareness that your editing may make or break someone else's career. No pressure or anything, right? The going rate for this is about $35 per page. Get a deposit of half up-front. Be prepared for a rough ride, and be patient with the student.

Other editing gigs for students can stray into a funky gray area. I've had a few students who really, really, really needed help with their writing. Editing wasn't even the word for what they needed. It was much more like a re-write.

That's where it got sticky. If I re-write an entire essay, it's my essay – not the student's work. I avoid situations like this like the plague.

Tips on Editing Jobs

It's best, if you do get an editing gig, to be very specific with the client about how much editing they want done. If all they want is a proofread, and you make any other changes, they'll be very unhappy. Most amateur writers are VERY sensitive about their words (oh heck, some pros are too!).

As you edit, use the Track Changes so your client can see every change you've made. If you're not familiar with that tool, check it out – it's very handy. There's also a comment function that lets you query the author.

I avoid editing projects that require me to handle actual paper. It's a lot more work to write with a red pen than it is to just type. It's your call, but remember to be as efficient as possible.

You'll need more technical knowledge in order to be a good editor. There are reference books to learn and consult, official styles to know, and a host of rules and editing marks and terms you might not know about on your own.

Get a copy of the Chicago Manual of Style, Strunk and White's *Elements of Style*, the Merriam-Webster Dictionary, and books on APA, AP, and AMA styles. When someone needs an editor, one of these styles is usually specified. It's something you can't fake, either!

You'll find these books under "Books Every Freelancer Should Own" on www.workingwriterhappywriter.com. Just one note – you don't need any of these for most commercial writing projects. With these projects, you can write by ear (that's one more reason to love them!).

Oh yes, one trick you don't want to fall for.

It's sneaky, but sometimes people will ask you to do a sample edit of a portion of their project. A few paragraphs are fine, but if they send an entire chapter, run! Think about it – all they have to do is have ten people do a sample edit on ten different chapters, and voila! The project is edited. And nobody got paid.

Very bad mojo.

Indexing

Indexing is kind of the ugly step-sister of editing.

Nearly every non-fiction book has an index in the back. Believe it or not, they're generally not computer-generated. A human being created and compiled it.

It's an art form unto itself, really. There are entire books written about indexing, and some state-of-the-art software that helps make the indexing process a little less tedious. I've done it, but didn't really like it. No advice for you whatsoever about what to charge, because I prefer a trip to the dentist to an indexing project. Some people like it, though, so give it a try.

ELL/ESL

It's the same thing, but has different names. It's writing materials for teachers of students whose first language is not English. This is a cross-breed between education and writing.

It's a lot more complicated than you'd think. Just think about how complex English is – all those rules and exceptions, tenses, and constructs. Throw in the fact that ELL students come from all over the world, with different language abilities in their first language and their second, and the fact that one single teacher may have to reach and teach several ELL students at the same time as he or she teaches the rest of the class – whew!

I have a couple of colleagues who do a LOT of ELL work. I do some because I've learned a lot from them and know I can ask for help if I get stuck. Maybe we'll get them on a training seminar and see what secrets they'll spill.

The good thing about ELL writing is that it pays very well. It's typically for big publishing houses, like McGraw Hill, Scholastic, and Houghton-Mifflin. They completely get the fact that it's hard to do, and know they have to pay well. The deadlines are usually very tight. The projects always seem overwhelming when you start. But it's very interesting work, and knowing it'll help a teacher teach and a student learn is very rewarding.

Speechwriting

One of my first gigs was a speech. Piece of cake, I thought. After all, my husband was a pastor, and he speaks every week! Boy was I wrong on that one. It's hard enough writing a speech for yourself to give. You know what you want to say, how to say it, what your strengths and weaknesses are as a speaker.

But to do it for someone else takes a lot of intuition.

I liken speechwriting to having someone describe a picture in their mind, then asking you to draw it. Not an easy task.

Now, obviously, there are lots of very talented speechwriters out there. And they do very well. The gigs you're most likely to find on a job board, though, are for very infrequent speakers. They need a toast, a graduation speech, a retirement roast. All of these things really do best if you actually know the person!

If you take on a speechwriting gig, do your best to get all the info you can up front.

- Talk to the client.

- Listen to how they speak.

- Do they have a sense of humor?

- Can they tell a story?

- What can they tell you about their vision for the speech?

Ask a LOT of questions. It's your only hope for delivering a speech they'll want to deliver.

Postcards: Earning More by Saying Less

Beginning freelance writers wonder how they'll ever produce enough text to meet the minimum word count their clients ordered. Experienced freelance writers begin to have the opposite problem – stopping! We've discussed some ways to "wrap it up" (and there are more tips and tricks featured on my blog).

When it comes to sales writing, there are two extremes that copywriters need to master. Long copy is one – typical of an online sales letter. On the other end of the text length spectrum is the marketing postcard.

Just a few reasons marketing postcards are great:

- Clients love them because it's an inexpensive way to launch a marketing campaign. The postage is still affordable. The printing costs are minimal. The return for their marketing dollars is excellent.

- 12 months in a year + holidays in every month = tons of opportunities to send out a great direct mail piece. Offer a special, and watch these little beauties ramp up your profits.

- Could A/B testing possibly get any easier? Do two versions of your postcard and see which gets better results.

And those are just some reasons clients love marketing postcards.

What about you as the freelance writer? How about:

- Your clients will love them, which means they'll love YOU. Clients are all about results, and if you can learn how to create winning direct mail postcards, you're going to deliver awesome results.

- They're fun! If you're a visual person at all, you know how effective a great photo or graphic can be. Even if you're not a graphic designer, which I am certainly not, you can work with images to create a great package. Just letting your mind connect the dots between what a client's offering and different directions you could go with the creative end is a lot of fun.

- They're quick! Once you get the inspiration for a great angle, it's really easy to put the rest of the piece together. There's not much room for a ton of text, so you've got to be concise; but the main thrust of your text is your headline and call to action, anyway.

I have a client, a printer who specializes in direct mail postcards. He works mostly with small businesses and runs regularly scheduled campaigns for them. He was really just looking for a copywriter for the text, but was thrilled when I offered to provide suggestions and examples for the images on the front. Made his life easier – and it wasn't much more work for me. Talk about a win for everyone!

You can find inexpensive stock photography images on sites like istockphoto.com and dreamstime.com. Just get the watermarked (free) version for your mock-up. Be sure to record the locator information so you or your client can find the image again.

Getting Into Print

OK, not like newsprint! I mean marketing materials.

If you're artsy at all on the computer, and you can handle a bit of design work, you can position yourself as a one-stop shop for marketing materials. You'd provide both the content and the design your clients need for their business cards, postcards, direct mail pieces, brochures, flyers, everything they need.

There are online printers you can use that do a fantastic job for a very reasonable price. One in particular I've used is Vista Print. They have a "Dealers" program that has worked really well for me. For a one-time fee of $50, you get access to lots of specials, better shipping rates, and no upload or PDF charges. I've been able to get all kinds of printed materials for my own business there, and while I don't specialize in doing it for other businesses, I have a few clients who ask for this.

So, How's YOUR Book Coming Along?

"Huh? I'm not writing a book," you say, "at least not my own, anyway."

Well, why on earth not? What, are you afraid of a little writing? Think you can't go the distance?

OK, that's probably enough taunting to get your feathers ruffled a little. But seriously, it's been said that everyone's got a book in them just waiting to be written. And as a freelance writer, who better to draw your book out than you?

Let's be really clear here: we're not talking about reverting to the old misconception that keeps many potential freelancers out of the game – that the only way to get paid to write is to write a best-selling novel.

We're assuming you've pushed past that limiting belief, and that you realize the earnings potential available as a pen for hire.

Instead, let's talk about five great reasons for working on your own book:

1. You can share your expertise – and everyone's an expert in some area. Think your expertise lies only in an area nobody would even care about? Guess again! Whether it's cleaning (check out Fly Lady's success), knitting (check out Jill Eaton and a hundred others), or even cooking on the grill (Bobby Flay) – there are hugely successful gurus out there writing and selling books.

2. You can grow your client base. What's your writing specialty? Write a mean SEO article? Why not write a little book about your method? You could give it away to clients or prospects.

3. You can build an info marketing empire. Create an assortment of info products at various price points – from a free report up to a full book or course. It takes time, and some work, of course. But as I've said a thousand times before, info marketing is a freelance writer's retirement plan.

4. You can leave a legacy. Even if you never market your book, there are people who'll consider it priceless. Write your memoir. Write a cookbook. Write a devotional. Write a family history. Both of my grandfathers wrote memoirs, and I value these books immensely. One is still alive (at 91 and counting!), but the other is gone. Having their words is precious to me. Do the same, and someone's going to feel the same about your work someday.

5. You can pursue your dream. Alright, so I lied – there's still that thing about writing a best-seller! But you know what? Books aren't usually written overnight, and if you want to do this someday, you might as well start now and do a bit every day. Just don't neglect your paying gigs.

The best way to get your book done is the same as the best way to eat an elephant – one bite at a time. Schedule some time every day to chip away at this mammoth task. Set the timer and work without interruption. You'll be amazed by how quickly your book takes shape.

Information Marketing

I saved my favorite for last. This one will be a whole book on its own soon.

This is where my business is growing most at this point. I asked my wonderful coach about getting into this industry, and she had just launched a coaching program for just that purpose. So, we worked together for a while. Then I took a course ($$$$$) with Derek Gehl's Internet Marketing Center. Then I found the program I really, really like – and recommend for anyone getting started. It's Nitro Marketing's Nitro Blueprint System. It goes step-by-step through the process, and I've had the privilege of talking with quite a few people who've used it to create awesome info marketing businesses. Plus, it's really pretty affordable – especially compared with some of the other alternatives.

What is info marketing?

Basically, people go to the Internet to learn about something. Could be anything from finding a great gift idea for Mother's Day to how to treat a bad case of poison ivy.

It's all on there somewhere. It's the information superhighway, after all.

So where does all of that information come from? Usually us! We're creating all this content for clients, and they're using it to make money.

When I first started doing content and SEO articles, I was always really curious. Why on earth did someone want 20 articles on custom maternity T-shirts? What was the point of that?

It's a little bit complicated, but essentially, the articles are intended to draw traffic to their website, to give some information, and eventually to result in a sale.

Why is this relevant? Well, for two reasons.

First, if you can learn all the tactics that are important to info marketers, you'll become a more valuable freelance writer, and you could build an entire business just writing for these clients.

Second, once you understand the potential of info marketing, you'll probably want to get into it too. It's a great way to build a relatively passive stream of income by doing something you already know how to do – write!

Chapter 9 – Growing the Business

Checklist for Growing Your Business

Once you get your writing business up and running, there are lots of things you can do to get it to grow. But you've got to get the pieces in place first. So, let's go through a little checklist to make sure you're ready for the next steps.

- o You've got an entity for your business. You're not getting paid under your own Social Security number, right? Because if you are, you can kiss about half of what you make goodbye.

- o You've got your pricing down to a science. You know what you'd charge for the most common projects you do, and you know how to figure out what you'd charge for a completely new kind of project.

- o You're bidding on projects online daily. I recommend about five bids a day when you're starting out. When you get a little busier, you'll bid a little less – but you won't stop completely, even when you're swamped.

- o You've ironed out the kinks in your bidding templates, and know you can customize them easily to really address what each potential client is looking for.

- o You've joined some kind of networking group (or made your own), and you attend regularly.

- o You've got a bookkeeper lined up to take over your accounting tasks.

- o You've got an assistant lined up to help with other tasks.

- o You've got marketing materials: business cards, post cards, brochures, website.

- o You're writing down everything you learn to master, to form a procedure manual.

- o You're keeping the best projects you do as samples for your portfolio.

Once you have these tasks down pat, you're ready to systematize your business a bit. It's kind of like building a sandcastle. At first, you're just heaping the sand into a pile. But for it to become any bigger, you've got to pat it down, straighten it up, and make sure the foundation is sturdy enough to support some vertical growth.

This is how it is when you're starting a freelance writing business.

It takes time to nail all these little pieces down, to learn how to market your business, to find gigs, to price them well, to get money coming in. Once you're doing all that, and seeing a pretty regular stream of income, it's time to get into some deeper planning and analysis. (Ugh – more math!)

Revenue Forecasting

This is a good kind of math, though – and you'll like it. You're going to do some revenue forecasting now. You'll need a spreadsheet. Set it up to look like this for each month:

Client	Job	Fee	Invoiced?	Paid?
Matt	10 Articles	$250	8/2/07	8/6/07
James	Press release	$100	8/15/07	8/15/07
Rosalynn	Mortgage ebook	$2500	Project in progress	
Dennis	2 articles	$50	8/10/07	8/11/07
Total		$2900		

How's Your Proposal System?

Wow, that's a pretty dull title, huh? Either my Starbucks buzz has worn off or it's just a topic that's just not that exciting (on the surface at least).

But once you give some thought to this question, you'll start getting more excited about it. You see, mastering the process for lining up writing gigs is a huge step toward making you more profitable as a freelance writer. If you flounder on this, you're hamstringing yourself on one of the most easily systematized tasks involved in running a freelance writing business. Perfecting your system is a giant leap toward making the highest, best use of your time.

Whether you get your work from freelance writing boards, discussion forums, cold calls, direct mail, or some other way, the time you spend seeking work – as opposed to producing work – is unpaid, and therefore something you want to do as efficiently as possible. Efficiency equals systems. Systems are the upside of "ruts" – ruts that serve you, as opposed to ruts that keep you stuck.

So, how's your system? Take just a minute to think about the procedure you follow from beginning to end from the time you go looking for work to the time you actually start working on a gig. Could you teach it to someone else? Could you hire someone to do it for you? Chances are that if you said something like, "No, it's too complicated," that it really IS too complicated.

To help you streamline and systematize this crucial part of your business, let's look at some questions.

- Where do you look for work?

- When do you look for work? Is it part of your daily routine? Something you do when you're out of work? Something you do when you get around to it?

- How do you recognize a project or client you'd like to work with?

- How do you evaluate whether the project is, in fact, a good match for you?

- How do you know what to charge?

- How do you know how long to expect a project to take?

- What samples will you send?

- What's the next step if the client wants to hire you?

- Do you require a deposit? An escrow payment?

- Do you have a contract you use?

- How do you keep track of the gigs you've pursued?

- Do you have a way to test and track your marketing efforts?

Yikes – it IS complicated!

How do you eat THIS elephant? The same way you tackle anything else that looks complex – one bite at a time. Break it down into manageable pieces and master each one in turn.

What's in it for you to create a proposal system? Well, think about tying your shoes. When you're just learning how to do this task, it seems really complicated, non-intuitive, and half the time, unsuccessful. Eventually you figure it out (or resign yourself to a life of Velcro) and it becomes so natural, so second-nature, that you can do it with your eyes closed. You can teach it to someone else. You can do it quickly, effectively, and reliably.

What would it do for your freelance writing business if your pursuit of work was quick, effective, and reliable? Why, that sounds like a cash machine to me! Pull the lever, and out pops money!

Your challenge, should you accept it, is to document and tweak your process for finding work. Make a flow chart, write bullet points, whatever it takes so that you end up with a system that runs like clockwork.

Setting SMART GOALS

You want to keep track of where you are during the month. From this, you'll be able to set some SMART goals as you move forward.

Please tell me you already know about SMART goals (how many articles does the typical freelance writer end up writing about this topic?!).

Just in case, SMART is specific, measurable, achievable, realistic, and time-bound. The idea is to set goals you can track, that you've got a good chance of achieving (without it being too easy), and ones where you know whether you've done it.

It's a lot easier to set revenue goals once you've got the rhythm of your business going. Otherwise, how do you know whether you should reasonably aim for $500, $5,000, or $50,000 a month? Once you've got a number – let's go with $5,000 a month – you do some guesswork about where that $5,000 will come from.

$5,000 =   200 articles at $25 each, OR

                 50 press releases at $100 each, OR

                 20 website home pages at $250 each, OR

                 2 e-books at $2,500 each

Remember, you're just guessing at this point.

You'll probably go after and get some mixture of projects that add up to your revenue goal. Keep track of the proposals you send out, the gigs you get in, and the payments you collect. This is not the time to shy away from numbers. This is the time to celebrate as you get closer and closer to hitting your revenue goal.

And then, once you hit it a couple of times, it's time to bump it up! Make the whole process as simple, streamlined, systematic, and predictable as you can. The goal is to have a cash machine! You know that if you put in a certain amount of effort, you'll get a certain amount of return on that investment.

Going Beyond a One-Man or One-Woman Business

One great book you should read is Michael Gerber's *The E-Myth Revisited*. It's all about structuring your business so that it can really take off, without you in the way!

Why grow?

One reason – you're going to want a life! Writers generally start the same way: looking for work. We wonder whether anyone would ever pay us for our words. Then we wonder how to find those people, how to do the work, how much to charge – all those basics have been covered in this book.

The truth is, if you do what you've read, you'll build a very solid little writing business – easily making a regular income. And life will be grand! You'll be free to work where and when you want, with clients you like, doing projects that are interesting.

The time will come (and pretty soon!), when you'll realize your limits.

- You can only write so much.

- You only want to work so much.

- You'll know other people who want to write, and want to help them.

- You'll have more work than you can do on your own.

- You'll have clients who love you, and who want you to write every word their business prints. But… you're only one person.

- You can only do so much.

- Your family would miss you – and you could easily work so much that you defeat the entire purpose of being a freelancer!

When you reach that point – and it could take a few months, or a year, or more, depending on the effort you put into building your business – you'll need to look for ways to continue growing while at the same time unhooking yourself from the chore of writing every word.

Also, if you're aiming for financial freedom for your family (and it's entirely possible), you have to keep in mind one of the biggest rules: Your success depends on how many other people you're able to help succeed.

It means playing a bigger, better game.

This doesn't mean becoming a workaholic who has permanent laptop lines on your legs, working your fingers to the bone. It becomes a matter of working smarter. It involves helping others learn what you've learned, giving them a chance to shine.

It's just something to keep in the back of your mind. The way you build your business right now is not the way it will ultimately look. When you're building from nothing, you have to get it up and going, bringing reliable income into your bank account. You have to learn how to do all the projects you want your business to be able to provide. But it won't stay this way forever.

Documentation = Liberty

Just the word "documentation" makes me think of past jobs I've had. There were software manuals, procedural manuals, standards, and other dry guides to follow – in every business from the bakery where I served cinnamon rolls as a teen, to the accounting office where I worked as a secretary and eventually a staff accountant.

Businesses run on systems. And systems require documentation so stuff can get done the right way no matter who's doing it.

Documentation accomplishes something we'll call the "brain dump" – getting what you do and what you know out of your own mind and into the mind of your teammates.

After you've been building your writing business for a while, you'll find that you know a lot of little things. How to write proposals, how to communicate with clients, how to save documents, how to send invoices, and a lot more. All these how-to's will become second nature to you.

But communicating them to someone else can be a challenge.

Training someone else to do these tasks is crucial to the growth of your business. Because of time constraints, you can only do so much – and if you can't effectively find, train, and utilize other people in your business, your business cannot grow.

One of my clients referred to this as "the pig in the python" and while it's kind of gross, it is definitely a good description.

My coach once told me that I am the point of failure in my business. (It's not as mean as it sounds!)

The point is, the more tasks I must personally do, the more my business is limited. There's only so much of me to go around, in other words.

So, training others in the systems I've developed is vital to growth, and eventually to being able to exit.

One thing I learned from the guys at Nitro Marketing (my mentors for information marketing) is step-by-step how to get this documentation done with as little pain as possible.

For any task you know you'll need to do more than once, follow this three-step process:

1. The first time you do it, learn it for yourself.

2. The second time, document how it's done.

3. The third time, teach it to someone else.

There are ways to make even that simple process easier, too.

You can use Camtasia, or Camstudio (fr.ee) to sort of make a film of your screen as you do something. Narrate as you do the task. Then share the video file with the person you're training.

Who's this person? Well, I recommend a virtual assistant. You can find one either among people you know, or do a search (on Guru or even Craig's List). The same can be done for eventually teaching other writers how you want projects done.

You don't even have to wait until these teammates are in place. In fact, I recommend creating this documentation before you need it!

Believe me, if you start doing this AS you build your business, you'll spare yourself many of the growing pains you'd have if you wait until it's already in full forward motion.

Never Stop Learning or Reading

In the meantime, you need to read and learn everything you can. For many of us, fiction is a delightful guilty pleasure. We dream of writing that novel, mystery, or book of poems. We love nothing better than curling up with a great book – a real page turner so compelling that you feel *for* the characters.

This is not at all what I'm talking about! Don't put away the pleasure reading completely – but take it for what it is – entertainment.

As you build your business, read books about building a business, marketing, management, goals, time mastery, networking, and other business theory books. Also read books about the technical end of business writing. Learn about sales writing, technical writing, overcoming writer's block, books on style and grammar.

Really learn your craft. If you want to see which books I specifically recommend, visit www.workingwriterhappywriter.com, and go to the page about books for writers. I've read many, many books, and recommend only the ones that have had the greatest impact on my business there.

5 Favors You Must Ask from Every Client

"What? Ask a client for a favor? Are you nuts?"

OK, first of all, they're not *really* favors. I just really liked the alliteration. But they are requests, and you might feel like you've got to ask before you'll get them. So, maybe *favor* isn't too far off the mark after all.

Second of all, about the "are you nuts?" part – well, maybe. But that's got nothing to do with this. Asking a client for something (in addition to your fee) can feel a little awkward at first. This is especially true if you're still working through issues about your value as a writer. If you feel like your time and talent aren't worth much, it's going to be hard to hold your head high enough to ask for anything. But that's a topic for another day.

We're going to look at what your existing client base – whether you've got one or one hundred – can give you that'll help you build a thriving business. It won't cost them a thing, but it'll do wonders for your bottom line.

Favor #1: May I add you to my client list?

To be honest, most clients will never even ask to see your client list – especially if the bulk of them are online. But whether you're finding your clients through a site like Guru, using a direct mail campaign, by networking, or some other way, a solid client list can go a long way to establish your credibility. If you've got a brochure or a website, those are great places to create a list of your satisfied clients.

You may have some clients refuse – generally only on ghostwriting projects where they'd rather not have their employer or publisher know they had help. But it never hurts to ask.

Favor #2: Would you please share your results?

Big time direct mail clients in particular want to see your copy conversion track record. They keep track of the effectiveness of every campaign they run, and are constantly looking to improve their conversion rate. (This involves math – sorry! It's a ratio comparing how many pieces were mailed to how many people took action.)

As a freelancer, you won't automatically be informed of these stats, because you're not in-house. You'll need to ask for them, and keep them. If you can show a high response rate to your copy, you've got a good shot at getting a copywriting project – online or off.

Favor #3: Would you please give me a testimonial?

If your client is happy with what you've created, they may even send a testimonial without you asking. All you have to do then is ask for permission to use it. If they don't offer it, you can easily ask by saying something like, "As I build my writing business, it would be so helpful to my prospective clients to hear about your experience in working with me. Would you mind sending me a few words I can use as a testimonial?" You can even write it for them and get their approval.

Favor #4: Would you please serve as a reference for me?

On Guru, it's really easy because a prospective client can just look at your feedback and ranking to see how well you've done with other clients. Offline, some clients will ask for references. You want to have a happy client's permission before sending prospects their way. Your references probably won't get many calls, but it's great to have them in place just in case.

Favor #5: Would you please pass my name along to anyone who might need some writing done?

It is the absolute best feeling to have a new client come to you because another client referred them to you. It's an honor and a privilege for someone to think that highly of your talent and skills that they'd put their own neck on the line to recommend you.

If you remember to ask these five favors, your client list will blossom and grow – and along with it, you'll build the thriving writing business of your dreams.

Driving with Your Foot on the Brake?

I remember first learning how to drive. Basically, I modeled my driving technique after the only thing I knew: bumper cars at Six Flags. If I remember correctly, there were two pedals. One to make you go; and one to make you stop. Actually, I'm not sure there was a brake, after all, which is probably fine since you can only go about 5 mph.

Anyhow, I can still picture my dad, white-knuckled and gripping the dashboard, his face filled with horror as he saw me using my left foot. It was not a stick shift car. My left foot should have been firmly planted over by the door.

But I was scared. I had seen that gory movie at Driver's Ed class. I knew what could happen if I got out of control. I was determined I would not go too fast.

I figured that if I had my foot on the brake, there was no way I'd lose control. Everybody would be safe. Nobody would get hurt.

Obviously, this is not the way to drive. Neither is any way to run your freelance writing business.

And this is a lesson, my friends, that I'm still learning.

You see, once you get started and the work starts to flood in, your panic will be transformed. You will go from worrying about not having enough work to wondering how on earth you get all this work done. If you're like me, you'll get yourself all worked up over it. Just suffer through a few all-nighters, and as you lick your wounds and detox from all that coffee, you'll swear to yourself that never again will you take on too much work.

However, I'm going to propose that this is one way of playing very small.

How many writers do you think are out there, who would be happy to take some of your overflow work? Maybe they're just getting started. Maybe they haven't learned how to effectively find work for themselves yet. Maybe they haven't bought my book! (Only partly kidding.)

So, what if instead of doing this as the Lone Ranger, you actually built a team?

Working with a team of writers is a great way to create a win for everyone. You can pursue work with the pedal to the metal. You can help provide for other writers. Together, you can deliver excellence to your clients.

One hurdle to building a team is getting past a scarcity mentality. If you're convinced that there is only so much work out there, what are the odds you will share it? Or, if you doubt that there is any other writer out there who could match your talent, how will you ever trust someone to write with you? (Who knew building a freelance writing business would become a personal development journey?)

First, a look at how your foot got on the brake in the first place. It probably got on there the same way mine did. Maybe you hired a coach, or maybe you got a great book about how to build a thriving writing business from nothing (wink, wink!). Whatever got you going, it didn't take long before you picked up speed – and getting writing gigs started becoming a regular part of your day.

Next thing you knew, you were in danger of getting more writing projects than you could personally handle. That out-of-control feeling is a surprise, and may just tempt you to slam on the brakes. After all, you don't want anybody getting hurt.

So how would it help you if you could bid with complete confidence that you could get the job done? What would happen to your business if you were marketing it regularly? What if you could tell your clients without a doubt that you could make their deadline? And what if you could help other writers along the way at the same time?

Now that might get you moving fast! A win for everyone: clients get their work on time, you have a steady stream of work, and you get a team of writers around you, who've got your back.

So now you've got a question: Where do you find these writers?

Actually, you've got a few questions.

How do you know whether the writer's any good? How do you pay them? What if they try to steal your client? What if they plagiarize? What if they just plain stink? Will they return the favor? Who should handle the client directly? (Once you start thinking about building a team, you'll have these and many, many other questions.)

Rather than just diving right in on where to find the writers, let's start at the beginning.

You've got to spend some time thinking about what's important to you in a writing partner. Is it speed? Do you want somebody who can beat even the tightest deadline? Are you looking for someone who matches your writing style? Are you looking for somebody in your time zone? Someone who can edit? Are you looking for someone cheap? Do you want a writer who can handle projects that you don't know how to do?

Not that you have to choose between these, but it's important to know your biggest priorities.

Your first task in building a team is to design it.

Spend a few minutes writing a description of your ideal team. Then turn this description into an application. Ask the questions you want to ask. Write a bit about your expectations, how you'd like to pay (Paypal, check, etc.), what information would be important to you in choosing a teammate, what kind of writing samples you'd like to see. All of this should go on your application.

Get this ready, and it'll serve as the first piece of your "building a team" system.

There are millions of people on the planet who can write, but not everyone is going to be a good match for your team. As you get started, you really only need one or two writers that you can trust to help you get the job done. Eventually you might decide to expand, which greatly increases your business's capacity.

So now that you know what you're looking for in a writer, the next step is to know where to look.

The good thing is that writers are constantly looking for work. So it's not like you have to pay a pilot to write your message in the sky, all you have to do is go where writers go. Chances are you'll find writers the same places you go looking for work.

Here's a list of places I have found great writers – some not so great ones, too, but all it takes is a few gems to build a powerful team.

- Guru.com

- Elance.com

- WAHM.com (go to the Moms Who Write board)

- Craigslist.org

- Backpage.com

- Kijiji.com

- Local networking events

A couple of tips on looking for writers for your team:

Be specific.

Now is your chance to explain exactly the qualifications and characteristics of your ideal writing partner. Do you want someone who submits work that's already been edited within an inch of its life? Is timeliness important? What about originality? Will your writing partner receive credit, or will it be a ghostwriting gig? Will your partner have contact with your client? Does your accountant prefer for you to work with somebody in the US? Do you want to be able to pay by PayPal, or some other way?

Lay your cards on the table. You want to start this writing partnership with good communication. The best way to do that is to be very explicit in your expectations.

Think long-term.

Don't focus on one particular project, but rather on finding a writer you can work with long-term. It's also best to go looking before you actually need somebody. You're a lot more likely to stick to your standards if you're not in panic mode with a deadline looming. It takes time to interview a writing partner and to review writing samples.

Even if you don't have work for your writing partner right away, it's bound to happen sooner or later. If your team is in place, it's like you're creating space for additional work to flow into your business.

Taxes

Unless you want to get into a bookkeeping nightmare, I recommend working with your writers as independent contractors. Pretty much any accountant will agree that getting into payroll, and all the regulations and rules and taxes involved in that is much more of a headache than it would be worth.

Independent contractors are responsible for their own taxes, insurance, and everything else. All you need to do is keep track of how much you paid them. At the beginning of next year, you'll furnish any writers you paid $600 or more with a 1099. In order to do this, you need to have all of your writers complete a form W9, which they can download from www.IRS.gov.

Payment

For most of the writers I work with, we handle invoicing and payment through PayPal.com. PayPal makes it really easy to pay them, and I can quickly download reports for my accountant. You'll need to establish in advance whether or your writers want to accept credit cards through PayPal because there is a fee for credit card payments.

The other way might want to work with payment is to use Guru.com. If the writers are registered on Guru, they benefit every time you pay them through that site. Yes, Guru does take a small bite out of the payment, but many writers consider that worthwhile because it continues to build their ranking.

Deadlines

One of the fears writers have about working with a team is that they're going to end up pulling an all-nighter because the other writer didn't submit work on time. This can happen. But it can also be prevented fairly easily.

Especially when you're just starting to work with a team, you want to build in some extra time. Figure out how much time it would take you, if you worked like a crazy person, to finish the project if everything else went to pot. That is the very latest deadline you want to give to your writing partner.

It's also a really good idea to start off small. I made this mistake early on. I worked with a writing partner on a full-length book. She blew the job. I had to rewrite all of it, and it was not fun. Thankfully, I learned my lesson the first time. Now when I'm working with a new writer, we'll start off with one article at a time.

The important thing to remember is that you're client really does not care what happened – they want on-time delivery. You are ultimately responsible for meeting the deadline.

Plagiarism & Stinkiness

Another big fear is that a writing partner will plagiarize or otherwise stink up a project, and leave you with a big mess on your hands.

This can happen.

Again, because you are ultimately responsible for the quality of the work you turn into your client, you need to plan ahead. Make it very clear at the outset that plagiarism will not be tolerated. Also make sure you request and review your writing partners' work samples. I've seen some samples that were so bad I knew it would never work. Better to know that at the beginning.

It's always a good idea to run your writing partners' work through Copyscape.com. There might not be anything more embarrassing than turning in work to client having them report back to you that it failed Copyscape. For five cents a search, you can protect your business and your reputation.

These are the biggest hurdles most writers face in building a writing team. They may be enough to keep you just writing on your own, and that's fine if that's what you want. It really all depends on your long-term vision for your business. If you're content to write for a little bit of extra income, you can absolutely do that on your own. If you have writing skills that are in high demand, especially for corporate clients, you can probably meet your writing income goals on your own without working all the time.

But those are not your only two options. If you build a team, your earnings potential is virtually unlimited – even if you're not Bob Bly! And you can still have a life, too.

Having Your Own Writing Business Is Great... But You Still Have a Boss (or 100!)

One big reason lots of freelance writers get started is the desire to work for themselves. I completely get this – in the beginning of this book I mentioned a bit about the last time I held a "job" – if you can call it that. It was a temp position at a local government agency. I knew it would only be a few days – but even those turned out to be plenty, thank you very much.

The night before I reported for duty, I got a call from my supervisor. She wanted to stress that appropriate dress was required (being in Florida, I can see her point – we tend to wear flip-flops everywhere), and that meant no belly shirts (I'm 40!), and that if I had any tattoos, they needed to be covered (um, okay). She also told me the name of the lady I'd need to check with if (IF!) I needed to use the restroom. That was the final straw. I needed the money, so yeah, I was going to take the assignment. But it got worse from there, and I decided enough was enough – time to be my own boss.

So I started a writing business.

And being new, I took gigs from anyone who'd hire me. (Sound familiar?) Unreasonable deadlines. Peanut-like pay. You name it, I accepted it, until I learned better.

Now my clients are generally pretty awesome. Most of them are repeats. Some have become delightful friends (even though we've never met!). But it's still a client and writer relationship. They place orders, and I fill them. Which means, essentially, I've got a bunch of bosses.

Contrast this with the other branch of my business, which is info marketing. Granted, it's squeezed into a couple of hours each day, but as it grows in profitability, it'll probably take over more of my workday.

I build my own websites (using XSite Pro – very easy), write my own copy, and develop my own products. On my own deadlines. According to specs I set. On topics I choose. See a pattern here?

Don't get me wrong – I'm incredibly grateful for my thriving writing business. It's rewarding to get paid to write. I've gotten to a place where my regular clients are awesome – practically hand-picked.

But I think every freelance writer needs to consider ways they can truly be their own boss, and that generally means learning about internet marketing – especially info marketing. There's a learning curve, of course. You've got software to learn, keyword research techniques, niche market research, marketing, formatting, delivery, and other details that can take a while to perfect.

That said, the years will pass by whether you jump in or not, and if you start learning now you could have a nice side business down the road. Success experts always stress the importance of developing multiple streams of income. Some suggest getting into a network marketing business (I tried this – miserable failure!). Others suggest getting into real estate investing (working on this in the Detroit area now – slow results, but promising, kind of stressful). Still others recommend playing around with the stock market (no thanks).

The options are out there, and definitely worth thinking about so you can find something that fits well. My writing business coach recommended info marketing to me over all of these though, and with a very reasonable explanation – control.

I figure I'll keep writing for clients for several more years. But at some point, like when I'm 80 and all arthritic, it'll lose its appeal. By then, I'm thinking these other branches of my business will be solid enough to support me into my old age. (Did I mention my family tends to live really, really, really long?)

Just some food for thought. Once you learn how to build a thriving writing business, you can use these same principles to create one successful business after another, and another.

Your Freelance Writing Business: How Will It End?

I think it's one of Stephen Covey's famous habits – but I've heard it so many places now that I'm not sure where it originated: Begin with the end in mind.

It's a little weird to think about the end of your freelance writing business, especially when you're just starting out. But it's actually a very valuable exercise, and something I've been doing a lot of thinking about lately as I plan for the future and expansion of my business.

This process is called exit strategy planning.

No matter whether you own a McDonalds, invest in real estate, play in the stock market, or any other kind of business, you're supposed to have an exit strategy. It's your plan for how it all ends, how you get out. The strategy you choose has a lot to do with how you build your business in the first place, and shapes the daily activities as well.

Basically, there are a few different strategies people look at:

- Selling

- Going passive

- Passing it on

- Fire sale

- Disappearing

The crown jewel is Door #1: Selling

Think about a little business that grows and flourishes, and then is bought for beaucoup bucks by an investor. Part of making this happen is putting in place effective systems that make your business run profitably with a minimum of dependence on your personal attention. They want to see financial statements and other proof that what they buy will survive after you're gone. Think of a McDonalds franchise, and you'll get the basic idea. The recipes in one are the same as in any other McDonalds anywhere (although there was some mysterious concoction at a McD's I visited in the Philippines several years ago).

Door #2: Going Passive

The passive route requires a lot of the same prep work as selling – except basically, you are the investor, and you don't pay yourself for your company. You just set the system in motion and step back. You guide a bit, correct and direct here and there, but aren't directly involved in the day-to-day operations. You just collect the profits. Nice!

Door #3: Passing It On

Passing it on doesn't seem to work too well. Having seen that plan in action in different organizations, I've got doubts about it ever working smoothly. It usually looks like this: Smith gets successful and wants to set up his sons in business. The shingle changes to read "Smith and Sons" – until Smith croaks, and then it's just "Sons." That's when the employees freak out because the sons are idiots and everything they touch turns to poo. They revolt because they can't stand it any longer. The business is gone within a couple of years.

Door #4 and #5: Fire Sale or Disappearing

The fire sale and its ugly cousin called disappearing, though, are the worst. Basically, something bad happens and the business owner wants to sell – but never planned for the systems that would make the business attractive to a buyer. Time runs out and either some crazy buyer picks it up for a pittance or the doors close without warning.

So, which one sounds best?

OK, that's a trick question. I'd take either of the first two, myself.

When I first brought up this discussion to a group of freelance writers, it became... well, I can only liken the discussion to poking a nest of giddy hornets.

You see, most freelance writers, when they're just starting out are so amazed to find themselves actually landing a client. It's a shock to the system to find out that your skills are actually valuable – after all, if it's so easy for you to write, isn't it like that for everyone?

We tend to think of high-paying careers as requiring a string of advanced degrees trailing after your last name, or some astonishing level of athletic ability, or a talent that's powerful enough to get you noticed in a coffee shop.

Baloney.

There's a tremendous – and always growing – market for writing. Coaching clients I've worked with are often startled to see how within a month or two of hanging their freelance writing shingle they're swamped. It always sounds the same, "You won't believe it, but I'm so busy I've got to turn down this new project!"

The thing is, unless you want to spend your golden years writing articles on the top seven tips for getting rid of dogs' bad breath, five green uses for plastic grocery bags, or press releases announcing the opening of the new car wash in your town, you need to have a plan to get out.

And if you're like me, you don't want to wait until you're old and gray.

In having this discussion, I've heard from writers all over the place weighing in on their top exit strategy choice. Overwhelmingly, they're choosing Door #1 or Door #2.

There's always the stunned silence at first, and I can hear the hamsters running on the wheels. "Huh! Never thought of my writing business as an investment not entirely unlike owning a McDonalds franchise." Then comes the dawn of realization: "Oh. My. Goodness. You mean I could build this up for a few years and then step back and let it run (and pay me), without me doing all/any of the writing?"

My next question is always this: So, what would you DO at that point? Some answers so far:

- Write a novel

- Do missions work

- Travel

- Invest in real estate

- Do it again, starting another business using what I learned

- Teach my kids how to do what I did (in principle) so they can build some kind of business of their own as they grow up

- Start a charitable foundation

And yes, I know that's possibly a scary question to answer – especially out loud. We're so conditioned to identifying ourselves by what we do for work, to filling our days with busy-ness, that it can be hard to even imagine liberty.

By the way, this is no "pie in the sky" aerie-fairy exercise. It's a fact. If you build a thriving writing business (even starting from nothing), it will become a reliable, productive asset that enables you to basically design your own life.

Once they wrap their minds around the possibilities inherent in Door #2, most writers recognize their writing business as the vehicles they are. With steady income coming in from a business that you don't have to spend all your time on, you're free to write that novel, travel, volunteer, or whatever else really lights your fire. Essentially, the goal is to get your business to the point where it can run without your hands-on attention – to make yourself replaceable.

So, how do you get from here to there?

No matter where you are on the path to Door #2 – whether you're just starting and haven't landed your first paying gig yet, or you're so busy writing that you can hardly see the light of day – you can stop right where you are to formulate a game plan that'll get you to your final destination as directly as possible.

"Do you want fries with that?"

Ever notice how wherever you go, even to the ends of the earth, if you go to a McDonalds, it's the same? Sure, in some more exotic locales, you might find some interesting extras on the menu. But a French fry is a French fry. Your burger is going to look and taste the same whether you get it in Vermont or Virginia, Oregon or Ohio.

No easy feat – at least without a system in place.

My grandmother used to make this amazing boiled custard at Christmas. (It's an acquired taste, I've been told.) I've got the recipe. I try it every year. But it's never the same as hers. Thinking back, I'm not sure she actually followed a strict recipe (at least not one that was written); after all, she'd made it so many times she could just do it from memory.

That kind of thing works great for family heirloom recipes – but not for your writing business. (Or for any other business, for that matter.)

Imagine going to a McDonalds and being surprised to find fat crinkle fries instead of the usual skinny, salty, crispy fries you're used to. What the heck? And what if you bit into your burger and found someone had gotten creative by adding chopped onion into the ground beef? Whoa. Freaky.

What's made McDonalds so successful is its systems. A fry is a fry is a fry. The franchise owner knows that the fry guy knows exactly how long they need to stay in the oil, how many shakes of salt, how long they can sit under the heat lamp. He's following a system, and just like pulling a lever on a machine, he knows what's going to come out. He can train a new worker, and know he'll get the same results. He can move across the country and follow the same system, and get the same results. All because of the system.

Now, of course a writing business is substantially different from a fast food joint. However, the idea of systems works the same way.

If you have a system for getting writing gigs, for project management, for getting the writing done, for collecting payment, for customer service, you can eventually make yourself replaceable (and thus free to go do whatever you really WANT to do). You can train someone to take over various tasks in your business, and know that as long as they follow the system, the output will be consistent. Your French fries will always be the same. You pull the lever, and out pops the result you're after.

How do you do that?

1. Start documenting your systems. As you do a routine task, take notes on exactly how you do it.

2. Check your work. The next time you do that task, follow your own notes to check their accuracy.

3. Test your system. Have someone else (a virtual assistant, a protégé, heck, even your spouse!) use your notes, with your supervision, to do that task. What happens?

4. Tweak it. If questions came up during the test, address them and clarify your documentation. Then try it again.

5. Replace yourself. Once you've got someone who can fry the fries, let them do it. Move on to another task and repeat the process.

By repeating this cycle of creating systems, setting them in motion, and moving up your own ladder, you'll make the highest, best use of your own time. At the same time, you put your business on the path to opening Door #2 – whatever that looks like for you.

Chapter 10 – The Mental Game of Writing

Chicken-hearted.

That's the best way I can describe how I entered the world of freelance writing.

With so many failed businesses in my wake, I was really scared that this would have the same fate. Suspecting that might be the same for you.

One thing I've discovered along the way, and you've seen it by now woven throughout these pages, is that the thing about accomplishing a goal that makes it so cool is who you become in the process.

To be honest, that's a journey I can't take for you – and I wouldn't want to. Uncovering all this for yourself is a huge gift you can give yourself.

However, I've written some pieces throughout the years about the mental end of starting a writing business. Based on the emails I've gotten, they've resonated with a lot of writers.

So I decided to include them in this second edition of my book. They're separate articles – so I'll keep them that way. I hope they help you as you take on that part of your business, too.

Take the Plunge – Courage Has Its Rewards

I was zipping along A1A in Key West at sunset on my hog (okay, actually it was a moped, but play along!). The breeze was delightful. The view was amazing. My son's death grip on my ribs had finally loosened once he realized he had a chance of surviving this adventure.

We'd gone along with my husband on a business trip – the best tag-along opportunity we'd ever had. And we'd decided to try something completely different.

No offense, but I've got to confess – I usually have a bit of judgment for people on motorcycles and mopeds. They seem crazy, cruising along with the traffic (including huge Hummers and buses and trucks) without any protection or airbags. I always kind of figured these were people who were less than responsible. (I know – it sounds pretty mean now that I see it on the page.)

So when the rest of the family suggested that we rent these mopeds, part of me balked. A big part. And when the moped rental guy gave us a quick lesson, I halfway wanted to say, "No thanks, I've changed my mind" and chicken out.

But then I took a moment to ask myself, "Who am I calling chicken?"

- The woman who built a thriving business doing something many other people only dream of doing?

- The woman who's traveled alone across the country to participate in leadership training seminars that left the old comfort zone in the dust.

- The woman who's partnering with some other amazing people to reshape neighborhoods and empower people through home ownership in Detroit?

- The woman who's living to set a good example of living as a Compassionate Samurai – stepping into courage, commitment, honor, contribution, trust, personal responsibility, knowledge, focus, abundance, and honesty?

Nope. That woman would not be afraid of a bike with a motor. That woman would seize the day. That woman would enjoy herself!

And you know what? It was so much fun that I'm angling to take our next vacation somewhere where we can ride mopeds! In fact, I'm close to becoming a moped freak! Hey, for $6, I drove that thing about 140 miles – quite a feat on a small island like that.

So how does this little anecdote apply to you?

Easy. You're doing something many people would think is really scary. Whether you're making a go of this business full-time or on the side, you're taking a risk. You could put your heart into your writing, and have it rejected. You could go for gigs and be told you're not good enough. You could stink as you start out.

Sure – lots of doom and gloom could happen.

Or, you could find that this is the profession you were created to do. You could find the pure joy of using your creative mind to earn an income. You could get to stay home with your kids. You could get so successful at this that you teach other people how to achieve the same liberty you enjoy. You could build satisfying relationships with clients who are so grateful for how you've helped them succeed. You could create financial freedom for your family. You could change the world – all because you had some courage.

So, to all those motorcycle people out there, I offer my heartfelt apologies for misunderstanding you. To all you burgeoning freelance writers out there, I honor you for your courage and determination. To my kids, I hope you'll be inspired by your old mom's daring do – and that you'll stop laughing at my moped hair.

Got a Big But?

Nope, I didn't leave out a 't' on that. And I'm not being fresh, either.

I'm talking about the one word that puts an immediate stop to your creativity, your problem-solving capabilities, and ultimately, your ability to reach your goals and dreams.

It's 'but'.

How's this happen? Let's take a look at a little example:

"Joanne" is a talented writer – I've seen her stuff, and she's got the goods. She's also got a 9 – 5 job that's sucking the lifeblood out of her. A demeaning, disrespectful boss, a long commute, and only enough time off to give her the chance to taste liberty and then have it torn from her grasp six days later. Oh yes, and she's got small kids at home who cry every day as she leaves, and are asleep many nights by the time she gets home.

Talking with her, I asked her to share her dreams and plans for the future. Might sound familiar to you.

"I'd love to build a thriving writing business, to be able to have the flexibility you have in where and when you work, to be home for my kids, and to earn enough to live – BUT" and the rest of that sentence, you can just fill in with your favorite dream-ender. It might involve fear, circumstance, or lack (of opportunity, support, skills, training, education, connections – the list is endless).

See, 'but' is a conversation ender. It's a way of excusing ourselves from the table. It feels like we've let ourselves off the hook – but only on the surface. Because now, you've got this unmet desire to do something, or have something, or be something – and by going to 'but' by definition, you've put that goal perpetually out of reach.

So what's the remedy for a big 'but'?

Another three-letter word that opens up all kinds of possibilities.

It's 'and'.

As in, "I'd love to (whatever) AND I need to find a solution to make it work."

See what happens? Just by changing the conversation from current circumstances to what might be possible once you identify a solution, you stay at the table. You're still in the game, and you set yourself up to use your creativity to move forward.

So, where's your biggest 'but'? How would it look if it became an 'and'?

There's a great little book that ties in well with this topic, and I recommend it because I've used it – and the seminars put on by the same company – and can only say, they've changed my life. From the growth of my writing business to the way my family interacts, to the friendships I've cultivated over the past year or two, the common thread is what I've learned and become, largely due to the impact of the books and seminars I've found through Klemmer & Associates. If you get "If How-To's Were Enough, We'd All Be Skinny, Rich, and Happy" I'd love to hear how it impacts you!

What's YOUR Vision?

Want to try something fun? Close your eyes, stand up, and start walking around. It won't be long before you'll whack your knee on a table, fall down some stairs, or at least bump into someone. What? That's not your idea of fun?

Well, to be honest, that doesn't sound like a barrel of monkeys to me, either. It's a lot more fun if you can see where you're going. You know if you're getting close, what you've got to do to move forward, and there are fewer injuries along the way!

Building a business – any kind of business – requires having a vision.

Now before you get all "stuck" trying to come up with the perfect mission statement for your business, take a deep breath and (as my daughter's friends say) "Chillax." It's not a huge task – and it's certainly not one that should knock you out of action while you ponder it.

It's kind of funny, but if you ask kids what they want, they'll have a list a mile long. Ask adults, and we usually have a hard time knowing or describing what we want. Is it because we've run into obstacles and decided to scale back our expectations? Could be. Are we afraid to dream big, because we don't want to face disappointment? Often.

But you know what? One of the very best parts of being a freelance writer is the freedom and hope that this business brings. So, it's time to start dreaming BIG and BOLD.

Think about it. In what other business can you set your own hours, find a crowd of clients who are looking to hire you (so even those of us who hate 'sales' can succeed), do work that uses your brain and your talents, and potentially make a very nice income? Oh yes, and all this with the bare minimum of overhead expenses.

So, what do you want? What do you want your writing business to achieve? What's the 'why' behind your work?

Give it some thought. Write it down. Then, if you're really brave, say it out loud – to someone. Don't worry about it sounding crazy, unrealistic, or even impossible. You want to hear my vision for my business? (It's big – I'm warning you!) I even named my business based on this vision.

Triumph Communications, LLC will enable me to achieve the following goals:

- Provide financial freedom for my family

- Enable us to live well AND donate 51% of our income to charity

- Provide opportunity and encouragement for others who want to experience the joy of finding and fulfilling their purpose

OK, I warned you – it probably sounds crazy. And I'll confess that it took a while before I could say these goals out loud without giggling. And we're not there… yet.

But having a really BIG vision does some good things:

- It keeps you focused and inspired

- It helps keep you going through obstacles

- It enables you to live "on purpose"

Take a few minutes each day to consider your vision for your business. Maybe you're just hoping to pay for some "extras" in your budget. Maybe you're trying to support a family. Maybe it's just a way to get paid for your creativity. Or, maybe you're looking to change the world. It's all good. But being aware of your purpose and vision makes it that much more doable.

So, Who Gets to Draw Your Box?

For argument's sake, let's say we all live in boxes. (Be patient, this is coming around to your freelance writing business soon!)

Some people's boxes are large, some are small, some misshapen. Our boxes largely determine what we'll do today, who we'll talk with, what we'll think about, how productive we'll be, and how we'll feel about it all. The funny thing is, our boxes determine all that – but they're also shaped by how those same elements played out in the past days, weeks, months, and years.

It's the epitome of self-fulfilling prophecy. You tell yourself you are a certain way, or have certain capabilities or limitations – and then lo and behold, you play it out just like you wrote it. Seems pretty straightforward, right? To move forward, to be, do, give, and have more, you have to talk to yourself in ways that serve you better.

That's all great – when it's a matter of you drawing your own box by how you talk to yourself. But what about when others try to draw your box, it can be another matter entirely.

Most freelance writers I know can point to a string of strange, unrelated, and unfulfilling or unsuccessful jobs or business endeavors trailing behind them like a red rag tied to a piece of really long lumber in the back of a pickup truck. Flapping in the breeze, these 'failures' warn everyone to keep their distance – you never know what this driver's going to do next, and you don't want to be in the fallout zone when the inevitable happens.

Sound familiar?

If you're just starting your freelance writing business, you're making a bold move. You're expanding your box, going in a new direction. You're not just coloring outside the lines – you're moving them entirely.

People may not like it. More than that, those people might be the ones you'd most expect to be excited, to "get it" that you've finally found the thing you love to do, that makes good use of your God-given talents, that allows you to have the flexibility and portability your life demands.

You might hear them grousing about this being your flavor of the month, warning that you'll starve to death, already turning you down for the loan they're so sure you'll be asking them for within a couple of months. And you could listen. You could resort to looking for a "real" job. You could analyze your options (yet again) and refuse to take action. You could erase your box's lines and draw it again – smaller.

Or, you could do something new. You could take action. You could commit yourself to creating your own opportunity, to building your business, to doing moment by moment the things that will push you forward. You could use their doom and gloom predictions to spur yourself onward.

Building a thriving writing business is NOT rocket science. It's not like winning the lottery (although sometimes it feels that good) – you do have to work, after all. If it's like anything, it's like building a machine, part by part. You design, you piece together, you test, you strengthen, you test again. Eventually, you can point to a machine that works reliably, effectively, profitably.

And it all begins with the drawing of a box.

Hey, Freelance Writer: Who Do You Think You Are?

Not to cause a run on the Yoplait yogurt across the country, but the answer to this question may lie in your grocery cart.

Huh?

OK. Here's the story of how an html disaster turned into an inspirational self-development piece.

I had just launched an affiliate program as part of one of my websites. And part of getting an affiliate program involves a tiny bit of html work. Not my strong suit – as I found out earlier this week. Apparently, when people buy an ebook, they actually want to receive it! Go figure. And when they don't, and when a merchant forgot to update her phone number in the Paypal contact screen, they're left with only one option – asking Paypal to intervene. Notifications are sent. Mortification sets in. Reparations are made.

Long story short, I had the serendipitous opportunity to connect with Angie Dixon, The Internet Copy Doctor, who was gracious enough not to call me a complete coding moron. Following is part of our exchange:

> *I'm looking forward to the book. I work on Elance, and I actually am one of the best writers, in addition to being one of the top as far as feedback. I just always undercharged. I've already had the courage to raise my rates because of your sales letter, and I'm so looking forward to your book. This week I'm doing a project creating a list of suggested book titles. I started to bid $577, which I thought was outrageous, and then bid $777--and GOT IT. I've written entire books for less than that!*

> *It really is amazing, considering last week I was still writing 10 articles for $57. I think I just needed a shot of confidence. I've been doing this 20 years; I ought to get paid well.*

> *It's wild how my thinking has changed. Last night I bought real Yoplait yogurt. I usually buy the Kroger brand at $0.44. Yoplait was on sale for $0.67, and I still stopped to think about it. Then I thought, "I'm not the person I was last week. I don't have to save $2.30 on ten tubs of yogurt." Funny how that works.*

Exactly – funny how that works! Did I do anything for Angie? Not really. (I mean, I'm proud of my copywriting on the letter, but basically it's just the story of my business.) Remember, she's only JUST gotten her hands on the book. We'll check in with her in a week or two.

What happened? A few things you can replicate:

- She took a chance. She named her price – willing to kiss a project goodbye, possibly – and got it. When's the last time you gave yourself a raise? If you're not making "enough" as a freelance writer, you don't have far to go to ask the boss for a raise! The market and your skills will determine the ceiling on your fees – don't lower it artificially.

- She took a shot. Of confidence, that is. Who do you think you are? What do you think you are worth? Are you a nickel and dime one-gig writer? Or are you a valuable marketing partner for your clients? Up for a challenge? One that'll feel silly until you really *get* it? Introduce yourself, out loud, in front of your bathroom mirror. Your introduction will sound something like, "My name is (name). I am a (adjective, adjective, and adjective) writer. I've got my choice of projects and clients, and I name my own price." Feeling really bold? Why not create a video of yourself doing this, and post a link to it on the WWHW blog.

- She took the plunge. Hey, we've all been there, counting pennies and settling for "good enough" (store brand yogurt in this case). Do you operate from a scarcity mindset – what if we run out? When you can turn the corner from seeing your resources and opportunities as being scarce (kind of like gas) to seeing them as being so abundant they're practically swirling around you (kind of like oxygen) you'll live differently. Not that you've got kiss generics goodbye – the point is being "at choice" about how you'll live. The action point here? Become aware of the opportunities you have every day. Take a look at what you choose and why.

So, a big thank you to Angie – for her graciousness, and for being the teacher of the moment. And now... I'm getting this ferocious craving for some Yoplait mango yogurt.

Conclusion – The End? Or, The Beginning?

Freelance writing is a business that appeals to people for many different reasons.

- It's a great opportunity for parents who want to be home with their children.

- It's a breath of hope for people who are tired of soul-sucking cubicle-bound jobs.

- It works well for people who are retired, but want to stay active and earn some money.

- It's ideal for people who've always dreamed of a writing career, but who haven't managed to write that best-seller yet.

Freelance writing gives you a way to work when and where you want, to work on projects that are nothing if not interesting, earning fees you set, working for clients you like – all while doing something that comes pretty naturally to you.

It's just a matter of getting going.

So, how does a writer get started?

How does someone get from wistful wishes about someday becoming a writer? It's really not that hard, if you'll take the guidance and advice of someone who's been there and done it.

There's a lot of free advice floating around out there – on blogs, forums, and online articles – and some of it's pretty good. But much of it's coming from people who are in the same position as you are – they're feeling their way along, not exactly sure they're doing it all the most efficient way possible.

(Be careful - some of these people even claim to be writing coaches!)

Sometimes, just having the chance to ask questions and get advice makes all the difference. If you could get access to other writers who have done what you're trying to do – and succeeded, what would that do for your level of optimism? Just knowing you're headed in the right direction is a huge boost to your motivation level.

The Mastermind Offer

That's why I'm going to make you an offer. I saved it for the end, because you really need to read all the pages that came before it. You'll need to be in activity, to have the motivation to get yourself going, and to demonstrate you've got the goods to take advantage of this offer.

What I'm offering is this: the Working Writer Happy Writer Mastermind Group. It's a six month process to help you get your writing business up and profitable. It shouldn't take even that long – even if you're starting from nothing.

If you qualify, you'll become part of a very small mastermind group that has one purpose – building a successful business.

Here's what you get as a member:

- Twice a month for several months, we'll have a one-hour group call. It'll address the practical steps involved in building a thriving writing business. You'll have homework. You'll have required reading. You'll be challenged to take the next step to advance your business – and we'll hold you to the commitments you choose to make in the process.

- Twice a month for six months, you'll have the opportunity to receive one-on-one coaching in our Working Writer Happy Writer coaching gym. This is a fifteen minute call that's laser-focused on you and your business.

- All calls will be recorded, and you'll have full access to the recording – for your own use.

- A special, members-only forum for chatting with the other members of the mastermind group. Get feedback and critiques on your writing, on your proposals and templates, on your website and marketing materials. Find other writers who have overflow work you can do – or who can help you with your overflow work.

- Once a month, you'll have exclusive access to a special speaker. We'll hear from other writers who are doing what you want to be doing, financial experts who can answer your questions, writers who specialize in projects you can learn to do, too, and more.

How do you get into the group?

I've found that most people *think* they'd like to start a business, but never get around to even *reading* anything about it.

You've obviously come further on the road by making it to this page in the book. Of those who buy and read a book, very few take the next step of *doing* something about it. Of those who are willing to do something, very few are willing to *commit their time or money* to making it work. This is where it gets tricky.

You see, there are lots of people out there who offer coaching programs – and they're probably very nice, very capable coaches. They're not writers, and they don't claim to be. They make their money from coaching.

This is not me.

I am a working writer. I could write day and night and never run out of projects. I followed the model my coach taught me, and it worked like magic. I've built a writing business – brick by brick – and it's changed my life.

I know that I'm not special in the universe, though – if it worked for me, there is no reason it wouldn't work for you.

As a busy writer and mom, I've learned to guard my time. There's very little "throw-away" time in my schedule. That's why I go about my coaching program a little differently than other coaches might.

Rather than trying to get as many clients as possible, I'm kind of going the opposite way. I want our time together to be as profitable as possible so that your life is changed by your writing business. So, each mastermind group is limited to six members. This means there's got to be some sort of selection process.

If you'd like more information about how to get into the next mastermind group, just email me at info@workingwriterhappywriter.com with "Mastermind" in the subject line. I'll send you all the details.

However you proceed in your business, I hope this book has been helpful to you.

Wishing you a thriving writing business, and the satisfaction of knowing you've built it yourself!

About the Author

After a long and strange string of jobs and careers, Sue LaPointe finally discovered the business of her dreams in freelance writing.

Like most aspiring writers, she'd always dismissed writing as a career. After all, what are the odds you'll write a bestselling novel? Or that enough magazines will publish your articles that you can earn a good living?

After reading Peter Bowerman's "Well-Fed Writer" series, the door to freelance writing opened a crack. After hiring a business coach to help her build a writing business, the door exploded off its hinges!

Through Loral Langemeier's Live Out Loud coaching program, Sue worked with ace coach, Robin M. Powers. In just six months, she built a thriving writing business from nothing. Within two years, her business went from being a single writer to a team of more than a dozen writers serving hundreds of clients.

With two children at home, Sue treasures the flexibility of being a freelance writer. It's this commitment to liberty that makes it so delightful to share this golden opportunity with others who want to build their own freelance writing business.

Sue lives in South Florida with Doug, her husband of 18 years, their two children, and a host of pets. They enjoy traveling - and as long as there's an internet connection, Sue is happy to run her business from anywhere in the world.

If you have found this book helpful in achieving your dreams...
whether to be able to stay home with your children,
to create an income that sets you free from cubicle life,
to get paid to do something you love...
you are invited to participate in

Project Liberty

During the beta phase of this book, a dozen writers used the Working Writer Happy Writer system to build thriving writing businesses of their own. They report being able to quit soul-sucking jobs, get out of debt, and stay home with their children.

Liberty is the ability to do what you want, when you want, where you want.

To whom much is given, much is expected.

It is in this spirit that I have shared all I know about freelance writing – that you may have liberty, no matter what the economy is doing.

If you've found this book helpful, you may know someone else who thirsts for liberty, too.

Please feel free to give this book to friends, family, even strangers – you never know whose life you may help to change. If you have a blog, podcast, or website, please consider mentioning or reviewing it. If you'd be interested in interviewing me, please contact me at info@workingwriterhappywriter.com.

To order more copies, visit www.triumphcom.com.

2289479